COVENTRY BUSES
1914–1946

DAVID HARVEY

AMBERLEY

Cover image above: AEC Y 4 (HP 449), one of seven such single-deck buses purchased in 1919, is at the terminus of the 1 route at Upper Stoke. This bus service had been introduced on 24 November 1919. The Hora B28R bodywork had a very long overhang.

Cover image below: Broadgate began at the top of Cross Cheaping, which led to the distant Burges at the bottom of the hill. This was the heart of Coventry city centre and was the focus of many of the tram and bus routes operated by the Corporation. Standing outside The Royal Vaults public house, and alongside tram 46, dating from 1913, is bus 49 (VC 6516), a Brush-bodied Maudslay ML7 six-wheeler that has arrived from Radford on the 2 service. The tram is working on the 7 route to Allesley.

First published 2015

Amberley Publishing
The Hill, Stroud
Gloucestershire, GL5 4EP

www.amberley-books.com

British Library Cataloguing in Publication Data.
A catalogue record for this book is available from the British Library.

ISBN 978 1 4456 4704 3 (print)
ISBN 978 1 4456 4705 0 (ebook)

Typeset in 10pt on 13pt Sabon.
Typesetting and Origination by Amberley Publishing.
Printed in the UK.

Contents

Introduction

This is the first part of a two volume work on the buses operated by Coventry Transport. This book covers the period from the short-lived services introduced in the weeks immediately before the First World War in 1914 until the last of the Second World War buses, delivered in March 1946. Many of the photographs were taken during the 1950s, a fascinating period for bus enthusiasts all over the country and especially in Coventry, where the last remnants of the pre-war buses were still being operated. Nearly all the wartime Utility bodied buses, albeit either rebuilt or rebodied, were in service and overlapped in service with the new post-war buses.

Two buses from the era covered by this volume have survived into preservation, these being 244 (EVC 244), a 1940 Daimler COG5/40 with a Park Royal B38F body, and 366 (EKV 966), a Daimler CWA6 dating from 1944 with 1951 Roe H31/27R bodywork. Both are splendidly preserved in the maroon and cream livery and are a tribute to the buses operated by Coventry Transport.

Acknowledgments

The author is grateful to the many photographers acknowledged in the text who have contributed to this volume. I sincerely thank all of those who are still alive for allowing me to use pictures, many of which were taken more than sixty years ago. Thanks are also due to the late A. A. Cooper, Roy Marshall and Alf Owen, who all printed photographs for me many years ago and generously gave permission for me to use their material. Where the photographer is not known, the photographs are credited to my own collection. The route maps were produced by the author. Special thanks are due to my wife Diana for her splendid proof reading.

The book would not have been possible without the continued encouragement given by Louis Archard, Amberley Publishing.

Brief History

Coventry Corporation purchased the 3' 6" gauge Coventry Electric Tramways Company on 1 January 1912. The Corporation inherited a system that had opened on 4 December 1895, operating over 12.87 miles of track with forty-two open-top four-wheel tramcars. The Corporation added a few extensions so that the maximum mileage of the system reached 13.68 miles. From 1913, new trams were regularly purchased, mainly with Brush-built bodies and Peckham P22 trucks. All these were top-covered but, because of Board of Trade regulations, had open balconies. Cars 69–73 were delivered in 1931 and were the last trams in the UK to be built with this antiquated layout.

The Coventry Transport tram system was gradually wound down throughout the 1930s. Tramway abandonment had begun in March 1932 with the Allesley tram service being closed and replaced by buses. Next to go was the Stoke via Ford Street trams in March 1936, while in April 1937 the Earlsdon tram service was abandoned, along with the railway station service in the following July. Although the Stoke via Payne's Lane tram service was reinstated in mid-August 1940, some thirty-nine weeks after it had originally been closed, the last trams were due to operate until 1942. The routes to Bedworth and Bell Green were still operating with a fleet of exactly fifty tramcars.

The 11-hour-long air raid of 14/15 November 1940 brought an immediate end to those plans. The loss of life was appalling, with an estimated 568 people killed and another 863 badly injured. The city centre was devastated, with many medieval half-timbered buildings and St Michael's Cathedral being destroyed. Damage to industry was colossal; the main Daimler factory at Radford, the Humber & Hillman works and the Alfred Herbert Ltd machine tool factory were totally destroyed, along with nine aircraft factories and two naval ordnance stores.

As if that wasn't bad enough, more than 4,300 homes in Coventry were either destroyed or made uninhabitable. So bad was the air raid that a large number of the population left the city to take shelter in the surrounding countryside. Amazingly no trams were destroyed in this air raid, but the infrastructure (power cables, track and overhead) was irreparably damaged and in December 1940 it was announced that the enforced closure of the surviving tram system would take place. A further air raid took place on 10 April 1941 when a further 451 people were killed and over 700 seriously injured.

Coventry City Transport began bus operations on 30 March 1914 with six vehicles built by the Coventry-based Maudslay Company. The route was to Upper Stoke, but this was a short-lived situation as the chassis were all impounded by the War Department. In 1919, services started again with AEC YC-type single-deckers that were introduced initially to be feeder vehicles to service the main road tram routes.

Gradually, throughout the 1920s there was a large increase in the numbers of new vehicles, with the emphasis on supporting local manufacturers such as the products of Maudslays. As that company lost its place in the PSV market, it was replaced after 1933 by Daimler, who held sway in the city until the end of municipal operation in Coventry in 1974.

Daimler provided Coventry Transport with their standard COG5 model, albeit latterly modified to accommodate sixty passengers, as well as producing the AEC oil-engined COA6 model exclusively for the undertaking. Throughout the 1930s the two main suppliers of coachwork were Brush of Loughborough and Metro-Cammell, based in Birmingham. By 1940 the Coventry bus fleet was among the most modern in Britain, with over 150 buses in service and orders already placed, ready to replace the last tram routes.

The events of the night of 14/15 November 1940, and of 8 and 10 April 1941, irreparably changed the face of Coventry, with an enormous loss of life, a huge amount of buildings and infrastructure destroyed, and the enforced closure of the surviving tram system. One result was a flood of buses coming to the city on loan, followed by the allocation by the MoWT of just over one hundred wartime Guy 'Arab' and Daimler CW type chassis to the municipality. These were allocated in order to serve the large numbers of former vehicle manufacturers based in the city who had turned over to making every conceivable type of war material. All these wartime buses were fitted with Ministry of Supply-styled Utility bodywork, which had to be rebuilt or replaced due to poor quality and unseasoned wood being used in their initial construction.

Ironically, by the time hostilities had ended in August 1945 the Coventry bus fleet was in remarkably good order, although the wartime buses were in a variety of liveries including light grey, dark grey, khaki grey, grey primer, red oxide and cream and variations of the standard fleet livery of maroon and cream. The number of buses in the fleet had increased to around 380 units, which, even allowing for the loss of the trams five years earlier, meant that the number of buses had almost doubled. After the war many of the pre-war Daimler COG5s and COA6s buses, especially those with Brush bodywork, were in need of structural repair and these were dealt with in-house at Keresley Works. The decision was made to rebuild all the bodies on the wartime bus fleet, but there were too many for the Corporation works to undertake, so from 1951 until 1953 the rebuilding was done either by Nudd Brothers & Lockyer at Kegworth or by S. H. Bond of Wythenshawe. The last of the pre-war buses were withdrawn in 1956, while the last wartime buses went in 1964.

General Managers

T. R. Whitehead 1912–1933.
R. A. Fearnley 1933–1962.
N. McDonald 1962–1969.
D. L. Hyde 1969–1974.

Depots/garages

Foleshill: 1884–1940 (trams).

Foleshill: 1940–1954 (buses).
Priestleys Bridge: 1899–1940 (trams). Afterwards it was used for bus repairs and some outdoor parking.
Harnall Lane: 1919 to 30 March 1986.(Buses). Even-numbered fleet buses. Built on same area of land as Priestleys Bridge Depot.
Sandy Lane: 1954 to 30 March 1986 (Buses). Odd-numbered fleet buses. Used as main works facilities from 1966.
Repair works: Watery Lane, Keresley 1942–1966.

CITY OF COVENTRY BUS AND TRAMCAR ROUTES 1937

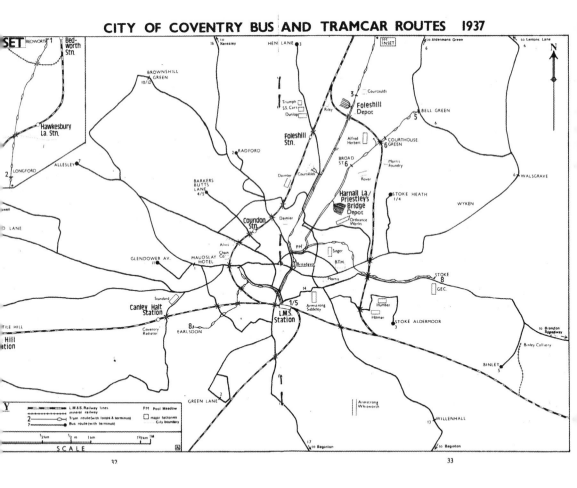

Early Bus Fleet 1914–1931

S 1057

Above: Coventry Motor Omnibus Company Ltd was set up in August 1907 with capital of £5,000. They owned two buses: one to be run between Broadgate and Earlsdon, and the other between the railway station and Canterbury Street. S 1057 was one of these buses and was a large chain-driven double-decker. Here, it has the destination High Street and appears to be waiting alongside the railway station. (D. R. Harvey Collection)

1 (DU 269)

Opposite above: On 30 March 1914, Coventry Corporation began operating its first bus service. This was between the Council House on Earl Street, the fire station and Stoke Heath to the north-east of the city. The Corporation began its operation of buses by supporting local industry; initially Maudslay was the chassis of choice, but after 1933 the allegiance was transferred to Daimler. The first buses were six Maudslay 40 hp vehicles with Brush H18/16RO bodywork, but their stay in Coventry was cut short by the outbreak of the First World War. All six chassis were impressed by the War Department in September 1914, and their bodies sold to Sheffield Corporation. Motorbus 1 (DU 269) stands at the Upper Stoke terminus not long after the new bus route was opened. (D. R. Harvey Collection)

6 (DU 263)

Below: A closer inspection of 6 (DU 263), the last of the Maudslay 40 hp buses, reveals the amount of municipal pride that was endowed to vehicles in Edwardian and pre-First World War days. Obviously cleaned for this official photograph, the paintwork on the bonnet positively gleams as the driver and conductor pose somewhat self-consciously for the photographer. The bus is standing on Walsgrave Road, quite near to Coventry City FC's ground at Highfield Road, with the typical late nineteenth-century houses found throughout the area serving as a backdrop to the bus. (Commercial postcard)

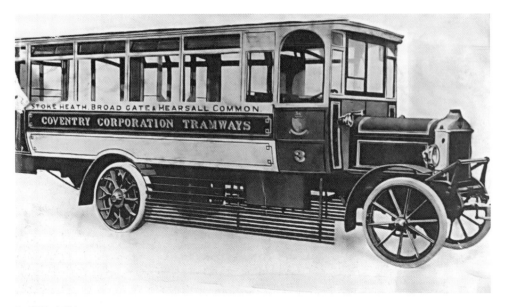

3 (HP 448)

Above: The resumption of motor bus operation after the end of the First World War began in November 1919, from Stoke Heath to the Council House on Earl Street, with an extension beyond Coventry railway station to Earlsdon via Warwick Road. These buses were also used in December 1919 from Radford to the Council House in the city centre. Seven AC Ys were purchased and were numbered 1–7 (HP 445–446/448–452). They had B28R bodies built by the Peckham-based coach builder E. & H. Hora. AEC Y type 3 (HP 448) was used as an official photograph and reveals a chassis with a high level frame that was little different from the famous pre-war B type. The 3-ton chassis was used initially as a military lorry, but continued in production and was also used as the basis of both single-deck and double-deck bus chassis. (D. R. Harvey Collection)

4 (HP 449)

Opposite above: The conductor, with his Bell Punch ticket machine, ticket rack and leather money satchel, and the driver pose at the front of AEC Y 4 (HP 449), one of seven such single-deck buses purchased in 1919, at the terminus of the 1 route at Upper Stoke. This bus service had been introduced on 24 November 1919. The Hora B28R bodywork had a very long rear overhang, which gave the buses a somewhat down-at-heel look about them. This bus was converted to run on pneumatic tyres in 1931 and was withdrawn in 1934. (A. J. Owen)

4 (HP 449)

Opposite below: Working on the 3 route along London Road in about 1927, with bunting hung across the road during a festival, is 4 (HP 449). This Hora-bodied AEC YC chassis was one of the first purchases after the end of the First World War and looked more like a lorry chassis than a vehicle intending to carry passengers. Crude as it was, it was used as a one-man-operated vehicle, and after conversion to pneumatic tyres managed another three years in service before being used as, at last, a Corporation lorry! (A. J. Owen)

5 (HP 450)

Above: Used by Coventry Corporation for the maintenance of its tramway system, HP 450, an AEC YC new in 1919 with a Hora B28F body, is seen soon after its conversion in 1931 to a mobile overhead tower wagon. Its conversion to pneumatic tyres had taken place when it was still a bus in 1928. As a tower wagon it had a crew of three. Although the smartly dressed man with a wing collar, a brass-buttoned waistcoat and a military-style cap was not one of them, he was probably their manager. (A. J. Owen)

8 (DU 1163)

Opposite above: The next batch of buses were numbered 8–11.These were Maudslay Subsidy A types. These had locally-constructed Hickman bodies, which had the usual numerous steps up into the saloon, caused by the high-level chassis. The bodies on these buses were substantially bigger, with a B36R layout, while the saloon height was slightly lower than the previous Daimlers. The first bus, 8, was delivered with the incorrect DU 1163 registration, but was given the missing HP 447 registration in 1919. (R. Marshall Collection)

9 (HP 2182)

Opposite below: Parked in Priestley's Bridge garage yard are three of the four Hickman-bodied Maudslay Subsidy A types of 1921. On the right is 9 (HP 2182), with the by now reregistered 8 (HP 447) to its left, and 10 (HP 2183) in the middle of the five buses. The remaining two buses are two of the 1919 AEC Y types with Hora bodies. The Corporation managed to squeeze more than twelve years of service out of the Maudslays, which was very good for buses of this vintage, with the last half of their service life seeing them running on pneumatic tyres. (A. J. Owen Collection)

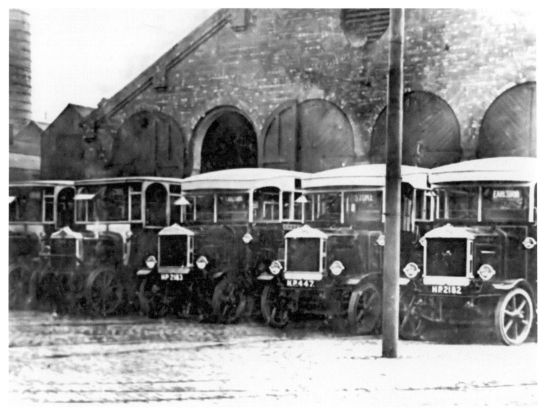

12 (HP 5744)

Above: The first double-decker bus, 12 (HP 5744), was delivered in 1923. It was a Maudslay CP four-wheel chassis with a full-front open-top fifty-eight-seat Hickman body. The CP chassis was originally developed as a seven-ton lorry chassis and this was one of only a few of these chassis to be bodied as a bus. Standing on Earl Street outside the Council House on its somewhat spindly rubber tyres and steel spoked wheels, it was an extremely ungainly looking vehicle. The body had the then usual outside staircase, giving the overall effect of a tramcar on wheels. (Southdown Enthusiasts Club)

15 (RW 1999)

Opposite above: In each of the years 1924 and 1925, a further pair of open-top, full-fronted, Hickman-bodied Maudslay CPs were delivered to the Corporation. 15 (RW 1999) was the first of the 1925 pair and is working on the Stoke Heath to Hearsall Common service, which was numbered 1. By the mid- to late 1920s, this bus route had become sufficiently popular that much larger buses were required to service the increase in passengers. These were the last open-top double-deckers new to the fleet. The next buses delivered to the Corporation had top covers, which must have been a great relief for the passengers during inclement weather! (A. J. Owen Collection)

16 (RW 1998)

Opposite below: 16 (RW 1998) looked a very odd vehicle. It was a Maudslay CP with a full-front, open-top, outside staircase body built by Hickman, a London coachbuilder based in Balham; 'Gateway To The South!', to quote Peter Sellers. The whole contraption looked like a shed on wheels and must have been a real trial for crews and the fifty-eight passengers who chose to travel on the bus. These were among the first double-decker buses operated by Coventry Transport, and 16 (RW 1998) is shown operating on the shortworking 4 route into the city from Stoke Heath. (D. R. Harvey Collection)

17 (RW 5000)

Above: In late 1925, Maudslay introduced a low-framed version of its double-deck chassis which was designated the CPL. The lower chassis height enabled the bodies to be fitted with, for the first time, top covers. Coventry Corporation bought three of this new model fitted with Hickman fifty-four-seat open-staircase bodies. The first of the trio was 17 (RW 5000), which is on the service to Upper Stoke. The hoarding alongside the bus, as well as advertising HP Sauce, Vim cleaning powder and Wright's cheese biscuits, is a play bill for the 1927 film *Lovers*. This romantic, silent MGM film starred Ramon Novarro and Alice Terry, and no known copies survive. (J. Stringer)

18 (RW 5001)

Above: Hamall Lane garage was opened on an adjacent site alongside Priestley's Bridge tram depot in 1919. Standing in the freshly painted Hamall Lane garage is 18 (RW 5001), one of the top-covered, Hickman-bodied Maudslay CPs of 1925. This was the middle one of the first three top-covered double-deckers in the Coventry bus fleet. They did retain an outside staircase, but the next deliveries of double-deckers, which arrived three years later, had enclosed staircases. Alongside it is an earlier open-top bus, which was the first Maudslay CP in the fleet. This is 12 (HP 5744), which was delivered in 1923 and survived until 1934, amazingly on its original rubber tyres. On the right is 43 (VC 5217), a 1930 six-wheel Maudslay ML7 with a sixty-seat Brush body. (D. R. Harvey Collection)

17 (RW 5000)

Opposite below: All the early Maudslay CP double-deckers entered service well before pneumatic tyres were allowed on such buses, so when the first buses arrived with more luxurious appointments such as a top deck cover, in some ways the new features only added to their antiquated appearance! 17 (RW 5000) stands at the Stoke Heath terminus of the 1 route on 2 October 1926. This Hickman-bodied bus was the first in the fleet to have a covered top deck and was about one year old when its crew posed with their bus. The driver had the luxury of a fully enclosed, full-fronted cab which from the side looked an ungainly afterthought and the passengers still had to endure a perilous climb up an outside staircase before reaching the safety of the enclosed upper saloon. It was quite surprising that the 1925 batch of Maudslay CPs managed to all achieve a nine-year service life, remaining on rubber tyres throughout their lives. The 1 route had been the first Coventry Transport bus route in 1914, but the commandeering of the bus fleet by the War Department at the beginning of the First World War meant that the service was abandoned after only few weeks of operation and was not resumed until November 1919, when single-decker buses were employed. (Pamlin Prints)

21 (WK 501)

Standing at the Shepherd and Shepherdess public house terminus of the 6 route in Keresley Road is 21 (WK 501), one of the 1927 Maudslay ML4As with a Hickman B26D body that had been delivered in March of that year and were the first buses in the Coventry Transport fleet to operate on pneumatic tyres. The bus looks quite modern from a distance, but the closer view reveals that they were rather like a large version of a vintage car. (D. R. Harvey Collection)

22 (WK 502)

The neat little twenty-six-seat Hickman bodies on the low-framed Maudslay ML4A chassis were introduced in March 1927, with a view to opening up parts of the city beyond the existing tram routes. 22 (WK 502) was the last of a trio of these twin-doored buses, which also had the distinction of being the first in the fleet to be delivered with pneumatic tyres. They could be used with or without a conductor and were at first operated on the new 6 service between Keresley Road, Radford, Gosford Green and Walsgrave. Strangely, these three buses (20–22) lasted longer, by up to three years, than some of the 1928 and 1929 ML4As, with 22 not being withdrawn until 1938. (D. R. Harvey Collection)

24 (WK 3102)

Right: The driver laconically leans on the front wing of his bus at the Walsgrave terminus of the 6 route. This service skirted the northern inner suburbs of Coventry and ran from Shepherd and Shepherdess in Keresley Village to Walsgrave, thus avoiding the central area. It had been introduced in March 1927 using a fleet of Maudslay ML4A single-deckers with low-built chassis numbered 23–25 (WK 3101–3), which were delivered in the following month for use as either crew or one-man-operated buses. (A. J. Owen)

26 (WK 6601)

Below: After another three Hickman-bodied Maudslay ML4As arrived in July 1927, another five similar buses were delivered in June 1928. 26 (WK 6601) was the first of this batch. These later buses had a separate destination number box and rear mudguard spats and, like the earlier ones, could be used as one-man-operated buses. This was because operating a single-decker with more than twenty-six seats was not allowed by the regulations of the day, so, although they could have sat thirty passengers, with the extra door they were within the legal requirements for being operated without a conductor. The bus is at Allesley working on the 8 route. This was one of several bus routes, including the 6 and 7, which were subjected to route alterations, amalgamations and extensions. (D. R. Harvey Collection)

28 (WK 6603)

Above: Standing outside Harnall Lane garage in about 1936 is 28 (WK 6603). This Maudslay ML4A had a dual-door, twenty-six-seater Hickman body which, because of licensing regulations, could be used as either a one-man bus or one using a conductor. The conductor carries his various accoutrements on leather straps, which were in use throughout the country. Driving one of these buses, taking fares and issuing tickets would have been a far harder job than it is today, so the driver must have been delighted to have been working on a duty that required a conductor. (A. J. Owen)

33 (WK 7503)

Opposite above: The opening of Corporation Street on 13 June 1931 was an occasion of great importance, and three special buses were used to carry the local civic dignitaries and their guests to the ceremonial event. The leading vehicle is 33 (WK 7503), a Maudslay ML4A with a Hickman B26D body dating from 1928. This is followed by Brush B26D-bodied Daimler CF6 47 (VC 1057), dating from August 1929, which was formerly a demonstrator from Daimler. This bus was the last full-sized normal control bus to be purchased by the undertaking after about a year on hire. The buses are doing a U-turn at the bottom of the Burges from Wells Street back into Corporation Street, with Hales Street to the right of the old grammar school and Bishop Street between the former Whitefriar's monastery chapel school buildings and the L. H. Fearis building in Wells Street. (A. J. Owen)

34 (VC 1784)

Below: Climbing up Trinity Street towards Broadgate is 1929 single-decker 34 (VC 1784), a Maudslay ML4C with a locally built Hickman B26D body. This bus was one of a pair of these normal control buses and was equipped with the larger 4.94-litre petrol engine. Neither of these Maudslay ML4Cs lasted very long in service, being withdrawn in 1935 and having a lifespan of barely a quarter of the tram it is approaching. The tram is car 57, a Brush-bodied fifty-seater mounted on Peckham P22 7' 6" wheelbase trucks built in 1921, and was one of the first five new 40 hp trams to enter service after the First World War. It is standing at the shelters at the top of Trinity Street. (R. Wilson)

36 (WK 7686)

Left: In November 1928, an improved version of the Maudslay double-decker appeared in the fleet. This was the CPL2 model, of which four were purchased. They had Vickers H24/24R bodies and were among the last bodies built by the company to their own designs. Vickers ceased body building in about 1930. These two-axle buses were operated on pneumatic tyres and had enclosed rear platforms and staircases. Numbered 36–39, they had 7.0 litre, four-cylinder, 72 bhp Maudslay petrol engines and for the first time had enclosed half-cab bodywork. Yet despite all these advanced features they were still quite an old chassis design, and as such had a short service life. 36 (VC 7686) was, along with the rest of the quartet, taken out of service in September 1936 and is standing withdrawn without destination number blinds, awaiting its fate. (D. R. Harvey Collection)

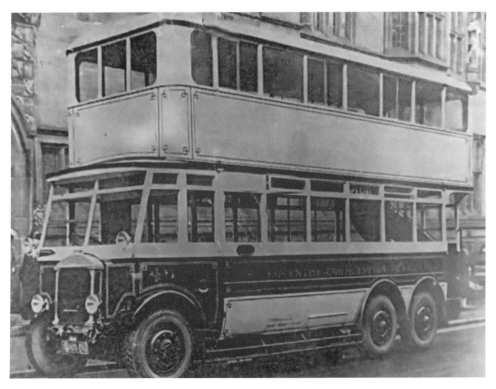

41 (VC 2632)

Above: The first production six-wheel Maudslay Magna ML7 double-decker was 41 (VC 2632). It is standing in the Brush bodybuilders' yard in Loughborough prior to delivery in December 1929. These Maudslays were impressive-looking vehicles and belonged to a fascinating transition period of body design. The enclosed driver's cab and rear platform and staircase were regarded as modern, but the cantrail lower-saloon ventilators harked back to earlier Edwardian tramway practice. The upper saloon accommodated thirty-three passengers despite not extending over the driver's cab; this was in order to relieve weight over the front axle. The bus remained in service until 1938. (Brush Engineering)

40 (WK 8765)

Opposite below: Coventry ordered seventeen six-wheel double-deck buses between 1929 and 1931. The large capacity of a 27' 6" was quite a tempting alternative to many municipal operators as it gave around twelve extra seats. Starting with Guy Motors in 1926, numerous chassis manufacturers produced six-wheel double-deck chassis. Karrier, Leyland Crossley and Maudslay all produced this apparently attractive new alternative, but only AEC with their large orders for their Renown model met with any degree of success. Most of the buses had problems with the drive line to the twin-back axles. Coventry ordered seventeen six-wheeled Maudslay ML7 chassis and these were unique to the municipality. The first one was numbered 40 (WK 8765) and had a sixty-seat body built by Brush which, with its full front, harked back to the earlier four-wheeled Maudslay CP6s of 1926. 40 also differed from the other ML7s by having the earlier, more vintage-looking, radiator. It is parked, when new in 1929, outside the Tudor-styled Council House on Earl Street, which opened on 11 June 1920. (D. R. Harvey Collection)

44 (VC 5218)

Above: Coventry City FC's ground was in Highfield Road, to the east of the city centre, and was opened in 1899 in an area of housing developed at the end of the nineteenth century. Standing on Swan Lane in the mid-1930s, awaiting football fans at the end of another home game, is 44 (VC 5218), one of the second batch of 1930-built Maudslay ML7 six-wheelers with Brush H33/27R bodywork. The bus is in the later maroon and cream livery, introduced after 1933. The bus is at the head of other Maudslay ML7s and is going to Jobs Lane, Tile Hill, to the west of the city centre. (A. J. Owen)

47 (VC 1057)

Opposite above: The three buses used for the opening ceremony of Corporation Street in June 1931 were led by 33 (WK 7503), a Maudslay ML4A, with 47 (VC 1057), the normal control Daimler CF6, sandwiched in the middle and followed by the almost new 54 (VC 6000), a Dennis EV with a Brush B32D body. All three buses were suitably decorated with municipal crests for the occasion. This bus was delivered in the red lake and cream livery, which was changed by Mr Fearnley to maroon and cream. (D. R. Harvey Collection)

49 (VC 6516)

Opposite below: Broadgate began at the top of Cross Cheaping, which led to the distant Burges at the bottom of the hill. This was the heart of Coventry city centre and was the focus of many of the tram and bus routes operated by the Corporation. Standing outside The Royal Vaults public house, and alongside tram 46, dating from 1913, is bus 49 (VC 6516), a Brush-bodied Maudslay ML7 six-wheeler that has arrived from Radford on the 2 service. The tram is working on the 7 route to Allesley.

    The bus is still in its original, predominantly cream, livery with red lake on the lower panels, dating the scene to 1932, not long before livery alterations and a move towards the maroon colour scheme favoured by Mr Fearnley, the Corporation's general manager, began. All the film billboards above the bus are for films made in 1931. These include *Heaven on Earth*, *The Mad Genius*, starring John Barrymore, and *The Rise of Helga*, a notorious film that was heavily censored and retitled from *Her Rise and Fall*. This was the only film in which Greta Garbo appeared with Clark Gable. (D. R. Harvey Collection)

50 (VC 6517)

Seven of the 1930 Maudslay ML7s were sold to Canvey & District in the spring of 1939, but were used for barely eighteen months before being laid aside. However, former Coventry bus 50 (VC 6517) survived in the Canvey Island area as a static caravan for many years, albeit cut down to a single-decker. The early post-war years saw many old redundant buses dragged to a cliff head, field or adjacent to a beach or even to some secluded riverside site for use as a caravan. They must have afforded a more luxurious and spacious holiday home than the tiny caravan on the next plot. (D. A. Jones)

54 (VC 6000)

54 (VC 6000), a Dennis EV with a Brush B32D body, stands outside the body-building factory of Brush in Loughborough. The comparatively modern appearance, for its time, of the Dennis EV hid that this model was, mechanically, almost the same as the Dennis E, which had originally been introduced in 1926. It had a 6.1-litre, 100-bhp, six-cylinder petrol engine and a cone clutch, and still retained a central throttle and a right-hand gate gearchange. This bus was the first single-decker with a half-cab in the fleet but, being a solitary example of the type in the fleet, was kept for only five years. (Brush Engineering)

51 (VC 6518)

Above: Parked near Harnall Lane garage when being employed on driver training duties is 51 (VC 6518). By 1939 the bus was in its last year of service, and by this time was being used on these auxiliary operations. Working on the principal of 'If you can drive this you can drive anything', 51 and its sisters quietly crunched their way around the city as the driver trainee struggled with an unsympathetic crash gearbox, sweated at his exertions at the steering wheel and wondered if the archaic mechanical brakes would pull up the bus in time. Meanwhile, the driving instructors, sitting in the lower saloon, would offer comments ranging from sagely offered advice to verbiage more suited to the barracks. (A. J. Owen)

55 (VC 9664)

Right: An example of every type of bus had to be submitted to the Board of Trade to be measured, weighed and tilt tested. In the United Kingdom, double-decker buses have to be capable of leaning, fully laden on top (usually with sand bags) to an angle of 28 degrees without toppling over before they are allowed on the road. 55 (VC 9664) is undergoing such a test at the Loughborough factory of Brush in October 1931. Despite the modern style of radiator, these six-wheeled chassis were rather dated as they had straight chassis frames, resulting in two steps on to the platform and into the lower saloon. (D. R. Harvey Collection)

55 (VC 9664)

Above: It was perhaps surprising that eleven of the obsolete Maudslay Magna ML7s were sold via Transport Vehicles (Daimler), who acted as a dealer, to Canvey & District. 55 (VC 9664) was new in October 1931, and while its Brush body looked slightly more modern, with a piano front incorporating the front destination box, it was still a mid-1920s body on a mid-1920s chassis. 55, repainted in the Canvey livery and edged in wartime blackout markings with a masked nearside headlight, was operated in the Essex area from April 1939 until October 1940. (D. R. Harvey Collection)

56 (VC 9665)

Above: After withdrawal in March 1939, 56 (VC 9665), along with the rest of the 55–58 batch of Brush-bodied Maudslay ML7 six-wheelers, was sold to Canvey & District, Canvey Island, where it ran only until October of the following year. 55 and 56, at least, were requisitioned by the Royal Navy. 56 was painted all-over grey and used to transport merchant seaman who were being trained to operate guns that were fitted from June 1939 to arm about 5,500 British merchant ships with an adequate defence against enemy submarines and aircraft.

These defensively equipped merchant ships (DEMS) were an Admiralty Trade Division plan that covered everything from the ships and the newly fitted guns, and the soldiers attached to the ships who manned the guns, to the shore establishments such as this one, 'at a port somewhere in England', and is being used to train crews for the Arctic convoys to Russia. (D. R. Harvey Collection)

56 (VC 9665)

Opposite below: The four Brush-bodied Maudslay Magna ML7s delivered in the autumn of 1931 had a more modern style of body, albeit still rather dated, and had a large seating capacity with a split of H33/27R. They did have piano front styling, but had very thick upper-saloon corner pillars and a roof that was extended beyond the flat-faced front windows. While the upper saloon of the bodies was modern and included drop ventilators and an enclosed staircase, the lower-saloon cantrail windows were more redolent of an Edwardian tramcar. 56 (VC 9665) is posed by the Corporation prior to entry into service. The six-wheeled Maudslay ML7 chassis was nominally given the name Magna. (CCT)

58 (VC 9667)

Above: Standing at the entrance to Harnall Lane bus garage in 1938 is Maudslay ML7 58 (VC 9667). The very dated Brush body design was actually impressive as it seemed to exaggerate the length of these six-wheelers and gave them the look of a stately passenger liner. The drivers of these leviathans, however, might not have been as enthusiastic as the steering was very hard work, especially when running with a full load of passengers. This was the last of seventeen six-wheeled ML7s and was fitted with a very thirsty Maudslay 7.5-litre petrol engine, a single-plate clutch and four-speed sliding mesh gearbox. The engines were notorious for leaking petrol and their fumes went right through the bus. (A. Ingram)

59 (KV 721)

Opposite below: What a contrast in Harnall Lane garage yard! Two virtually brand new Daimler CP6s, 110 (KV 7110) and 105 (KV 7105), dating from 1934 stand in the yard and make 59 (KV 721), a two-year-old, two-axle Maudslay ML7, look positively ancient. The Brush body on the Maudslay is of a design that dated from the late 1920s and had cantrail lower saloon windows à la tramcar and thick corner pillars on the upper saloon windows as well as a semi-piano front above the enclosed driver's cab. The three Maudslay ML7s, of which 59 was the first, were surprisingly long-lived with 59 not being withdrawn until 1945; even then it was sold to the Belgian Economic Mission and exported to war-riven Belgian for use until new buses could be delivered. (A. J. Owen)

60 (KV 722)

Above: In the spring of 1932, three four-wheel Maudslay ML7s were delivered and were numbered 59 to 61. This four-wheeled version of the ML7 chassis had the name Majestic, though this was rarely used. These had a much lower chassis and as a result were, in theory, a much more modern chassis, which was reflected in the batch surviving until either 1945 or 1946. The Brush bodies were similar, though lower, than the six-wheel ML7s and had a H26/24R seating capacity. 60 (KV 722), working on the 5 route to Barkers Butts Lane, stands on High Street outside the premises of Lloyds Bank. It was designed with a classical giant arch, built in 1932, and was one of the few buildings near to High Street and Broadgate crossroads to survive wartime destruction. This Maudslay double-decker bus was sold to a Coventry dealer called Roach in September 1945 but survived in their yard until 1960. (R. T. Wilson)

61 (KV 723)

Above: Four-wheel Maudslay ML7, with a Brush body, 61 (KV 723), is working on the 11 bus route, which had been introduced in March 1932. This bus service was introduced at the same time that the Allesley Road trams were replaced; it turned off the main road and into Maudslay Road, where it served the Standard Motor Company car works. Beyond that it passed along Whoberley Avenue before terminating in Glendower Avenue. This outer part of the bus route was lined with late Victorian houses which gradually gave way to early 1920s semi-detached residences. The bus is travelling into the city where it will terminate in Pool Meadow. (A. J. Owen)

63 (KV 725)

Above: Parked in front of Harnall Lane garage is 63 (KV 725), the second of the pair of 1932-built Brush-bodied Dennis Lance IIs. Coventry Corporation's general manager was Mr T. R. Whitehead, who is standing in front of the Dennis. Mr Whitehead was in office from 1912, when the Corporation first began to operate tramcar services, until his retirement in 1933. He was somewhat conservative in his bus requirements, and so the bodywork he specified to be built by Brush were outdated even when they were new. The thick upper-saloon corner pillars, piano front and the tramway-style lower-saloon ventilators made them look antiquated when compared to buses being delivered elsewhere in the country. Alongside are Maudslay ML7 six-wheelers 49 (VC 6517) and 51 (VC 6518), which looked much older than their 1930 delivery date. (T. R. Whitehead)

62 (KV 724)

Opposite below: Although unable to complete with either the contemporary AEC Regent 661 or the Leyland Titan TD1 or TD2, a number of bus manufacturers did begin to manufacture low-height double-deck bus chassis. One of these was Dennis Brothers of Guildford, who developed their Lance model. The Lance was very popular with the local operator Aldershot & District, but developed a niche market in the West Midlands with both Walsall and West Bromwich ordering the model. A pair of Lance IIs were delivered in 1932 and fitted with the same type of Brush body that had been fitted to the earlier trio of Maudslay ML7s. 62 (KV 724) stands at the 1 route terminus when virtually new, with its driver and conductor posing alongside the radiator. (A. J. Owen)

65 (KV 727)

This small Dennis 30 cwt single-decker had a 2.72-litre petrol engine and Brush B14F bodywork. 65 (KV 727) was bought in 1932 to open the new 10 route to Brownshill Green, which was introduced in March of that year. This service ran through the then rural area between Allesley and Brownshill Green, travelling along some very narrow country lanes. As the Daimler factory in Brown's Lane developed, these fourteen-seaters proved to have insufficient seating capacity by 1935 and were replaced by the three Leyland KPO2 Cubs, though even they were barely adequate for the increasing numbers of passengers. (R. H. G. Simpson)

Pre-war Expansion
1933–1941

6 (KV 64)

6 (KV 64) was used as a demonstrator for Transport Vehicles (Daimler) Limited and was
new in December 1931. It ran as Ashton-under-Lyne Corporation as their fleet number 6 in
1932 for several months and then returned to Transport Vehicles (Daimler) Limited before
being hired out to Coventry Corporation in 1933. It was fitted with an AEC A171F 7.57-litre
engine in 1934, becoming the prototype COA6. It was purchased by Coventry Corporation in
February 1936, having been given the same fleet number of 6, and was reseated to H27/26R
in September 1939. It was given the more logical fleet number 266 in February 1946 and was
withdrawn in 1949. The Weymann body style had the semblance of a piano front profile and
an exaggerated protruding destination box, which rather detracted from its otherwise modern
appearance. (R. H. G. Simpson)

102 (KV 7102)

Above: Working on the 2 route on its way to Green Lane in the summer of 1934 is the second of the Brush-bodied Daimler CP6s 102 (KV 7102). It was obviously a hot day as the driver has opened his windscreen and all the half-drop saloon windows are wide open. In 1939, as in 1934 and 1935, deliveries of buses to Coventry Transport had their seating capacities increased by three to H27/26R. 102 was withdrawn in 1948 but had been repainted in the post-war livery, which had maroon saloon pillars. (R. Wilson)

107 (KV 7107)

Above: Posed with route number 3 on the blind, 107 (KV 7107), Brush-bodied Daimler CP6, positively gleams in the January sunshine of 1934. The use of the Daimler petrol engine was perhaps a retrograde step, remedied the following November when three Daimler COA6s, which had diesel engines, were delivered. The 'P' in the designation CP6 stood for its Poppet valves and could achieve over 6 mpg. This was coupled to a Wilson preselector epicyclic gearboxes, which made the driver's job much easier. (Brush)

101 (KV 7101)

Opposite above: January 1934 saw the introduction of the first buses built to the specification of Mr Ronald Fearnley, who was the new incumbent general manager. These were sixteen composite-construction Brush H26/24R bodied Daimler CP6 double-deckers and were as up-to-date as anything else in the country. They replaced all the buses purchased before 1926. The first of the batch was 101 (KV 7101) and, like the rest of the batch, had a Daimler 6.561-litre petrol engine. The clean lines of the body was enhanced by side-by-side equal size destination boxes and Mr Fearnley's new maroon and cream livery. (CCT)

117 (KV 9117)

Above: Standing in Pool Meadow bus station when operating on the 8 route to Beech Tree Avenue in Tile Hill is 117 (KV 9117). This was the first production Daimler COA6 chassis and had an AEC A165 8.8 litre indirect injection oil engine, a type of engine introduced by AEC in May 1932. The Metro-Cammell body was the first of that manufacturer's products to be ordered by Coventry Transport, and the trio numbered 117–119 were the first metal-framed bodies in the fleet. 189 (CWK 189), built in 1938, is parked at the 10 route bus shelter and was another COA6, but with a Brush body. (D. R. Harvey Collection)

108 (KV 7108)

Opposite above: 108 (KV 7108) stands in Ford Street in early 1950. This was the oldest bus to need one of the five new Brush H31/29R bodies after air-raid damage on 14 November 1940, and it re-entered service in May 1942. It had sliding saloon ventilators instead of half-drop windows and had the characteristic Coventry-styled curved front and rear window panelling. It continued to run with a petrol engine until 1945, when a Gardner 5LW unit was fitted from one of the four COG5/60s re-engined in 1945 with the new Daimler CD6 8.6 litre engine; thus 108 became a Daimler COG5. It was renumbered 408 in 1949 and survived in service until 1952. (A. A. Cooper)

111 (KV 711)

Opposite below: Passing the old fire station in Hales Street, with the Coventry Hippodrome on the left, is 111 (KV 711). Delivered in January 1934, this was a Daimler CP6 and had a Brush H26/24R body. These buses were among the last to be delivered with petrol engines and, as they were coupled to a fluid flywheel and a Wilson preselector gearbox, it was perhaps a pity that they were never converted to oil engines. Only 108, after being rebodied by Brush, was converted to be powered by a Gardner 5LW engine. Perhaps as attractive as the original Brush bodies appeared, they were not considered for rebuilding or being fitted with oil engines. (A. J. Owen)

119 (KV 9119)

Left: Loading up with passengers on Trinity Street in about 1938 is 119 (KV 9119), the last of the three Metro-Cammell-bodied Daimler COA6s. All had long lives, not being taken out of service until 1951. The bus is going to Coventry railway station and its large number of intending passengers are being shepherded by a policeman. In the background is part of the Owen Owen building, which was opened in 1937 and guttered in the blitz attack on Coventry in November 1940. Although the rear of the body of 119 presents a modern aspect, the high-mounted rear side light, the red triangular stop light and the heavily radiused rear platform window are all typical features of a bus built in the mid-1930s. (A. J. Owen)

119 (KV 9119)

Above: 119 (KV 9119) was one of the Metro-Cammell-bodied Daimler COA6s that entered service in November of 1934. These three COA6s were the only ones built with the large 8.8-litre oil engine as all further deliveries had the smaller 7.57-litre unit. 119 stands in Pool Meadow bus station on 18 November 1950 with wartime bus 317 (EKV 817), a Daimler CWG5 with a Duple UH30/26R body, parked behind it. This CWG5 had received the post-war twin front destination boxes only about two years earlier, and would have to wait until 1953 before it was completely rebuilt by Bond of Wythenshawe. (A. A. Cooper)

118 (KV 9118)

Opposite above: One of the first three diesel-engined buses, Brush-bodied Daimler COA6 118 (KV 9118) is picking up passengers at the top of Cross Cheaping on service 2 to Redford in 1938. The buildings behind the bus were all destroyed in the air raid of 14 November 1940. The Coventry-style body looked well-proportioned from this angle and reveals that, when new, the staircase window could be slid open to serve as a direction signalling window by the conductor. This was in the days when trafficators were a luxury and hand signals were required. (R. T. Wilson)

10 (VC 5615)

Above: Standing in Pool Meadow bus station in about 1935 is Dennis GL 10 (VC 5615). This little Brush-bodied twenty-seater was built in 1930 and was taken over in 1934 when the Corporation acquired the works service of W. Duckham. It is working on the 2 route to Brownshill Green and remained in service with the Corporation, whereupon it was sold to Evans of Porth in the Rhondda Valley. (D. R. Harvey Collection)

121 (KV 9121)

Opposite above: Also delivered in November 1934 were the last petrol-engined buses delivered to Coventry, with chassis numbers in the same sequence as the trail-blazing COA6s. The Brush bodies were the last composite ones built for the undertaking as everything ordered up to 1942, when wartime composite bodies were the only ones available (be they bodied by Brush or Metro-Cammell), were metal-framed. Very similar to the earlier large batch of CP6s, these buses did have three chromed bumpers on the offside rear panelling. (Brush)

100 (VC 7519)

Opposite below: One of the more elusive buses was Coventry's 100 (VC 7519). This was a 5.6-litre petrol-engined Daimler CH6 and was completed in February 1931. It was fitted with one of the last bodies built by Depression-victim coachbuilder John Buckingham, with a H26/24R seating layout. They were based in Bradford Street in Birmingham

The bus was initially registered DH 8638 for demonstration to Walsall Corporation, serving for about a week as their 100 in March of the same year. Numbered 100 for the second time, it was demonstrated to Birmingham Corporation as their 100 between early March 1931 and the end of June 1934. It then arrived on hire to Coventry City Transport, numbered 100 for the third time, from May 1935 until burnt out in 1938. 100 is in High Street at the stop used by the service to Coundon beyond the policeman on point duty. On the right is the National Provincial Bank and Lloyd's Bank, both of which were built in the early 1930s and amazingly survived the wartime air raids.

A Bedford 3-ton lorry comes out of Greyfriars Lane while one of the 64–68 English Electric top-covered trams of 1929 is leaving Broadgate for the railway station. (Commercial Postcard)

123 (AVC 123)

Above: The devastation in the Broadgate area of the city centre caused by the air raid of 14 November 1940 was truly horrendous. By 1947 the worst of the bombed buildings had been removed, but there were buildings that still stood as gaunt shells awaiting demolition while town planners began to draw up plans for rebuilding Broadgate. The buildings in the distant Hereford Street, including the Greek porticoed National Provincial Bank, built in 1930, survived the destruction. In the foreground is the first production Daimler COA6. This was 123 (AVC 123) with an MCCW H26/24R body of 1935 and is working on the Longford service. Parked at the distant bus shelters is 148 (CWK 148), a Brush-bodied COA6 of 1936. (Commercial Postcard)

126 (AVC 126)

Above: Parked in Binley when working on the 5 service in 1938 is 126 (AVC 126), one of the twenty Metro-Cammell-bodied Daimler COA6 delivered during the previous November. During the Blitz on Coventry in November 1940, only, surprisingly, three buses were considered as write-offs, these being 128 and 183 with 167 being destroyed on heavy raid in 8 April 1941. 126 was damaged in the air raids of April 1941 and a virtually new chassis was reconstructed from its own remains and parts from 128 and 167. It was then one of the seven buses rebodied with a new Brush H31/29R body, re-entering service in May 1942. (D. R. Harvey Collection)

125 (AVC 125)

Opposite below: Wearing the post-war livery which had maroon-painted upper-saloon window pillars, 125 (AVC 125), a Daimler COA6 with a Metro-Cammell H26/24R body, was delivered in October 1935. As with all of this batch of twenty buses, it was reseated to H27/26R in 1939 and its original AEC A171F 7.57 litre direct injection diesel engine was replaced by the AEC A173 indirect injection engine. The pre-war body characteristics peculiar to Coventry's requirements were the built-in sun visor over the cab, the slotted pair of ventilators in the cab door and the post-war modification of having the staircase window made of 'modesty protecting' smoked glass. (J. Cull)

127 (AVC 127)

Above: Standing outside the unfinished Broadgate House in September 1951, when about to work on a football special, is 127 (AVC 127), another of the 1935 batch of Daimler COA6s with MCCW metal-framed H26/24R bodies. Construction of Broadgate House began in 1948 and it was opened in 1953, becoming the first new building in the rebuilt Broadgate to be completed. The bus, renumbered 427 in 1950, was to remain in service until 1952, whereupon it was sold to Birds of Stratford, where it was quickly broken up. (A. A. Cooper)

130 (AVC 130)
Above: Working on the 20 Bedworth service is 130 (AVC 130), one of the twenty first-production Daimler COA6 chassis of 1935 with MCCW H26/24R bodywork. It is 15 May 1944 and although the bombing of Coventry had come to an end, the bus is painted in all-over grey. This is not, however, due to any further need for camouflage, but because there was no maroon paint or pigment available and grey was the only alternative. The grey livery was introduced for pre-war bus repaints in 1942 and, until normal fleet livery was reintroduced in late 1943, twenty-five buses were thus painted, plus three of the hired Great Yarmouth vehicles. The bus is still fitted with wartime headlight masks. This bus was one of many of the 1949 and 1950 withdrawals to have their seats reused in the rebuilding of the wartime bodies on the later Daimler CWA6 and Guy Arab chassis (J. Cull)

129 (AVC 129)
Opposite below: Another of the April 1941 raid victims was 129 (AVC 129). It is standing outside the temporary shops in Broadgate in 1949 when working on the 16 service to Green Lane. Rebodied by Brush to the same peacetime appearance as the final style of pre-war Coventry specification body, it re-entered service in April 1942. The new bodies, of which there were five, all had a deep roof profile, a curved front profile and the curved up-turn to the end windows in each saloon. This took years off them all, making them look more up-to-date. Despite their comparative newness, three of them, including 129, only lasted until 1949, suggesting that all was not well with the wartime body materials. (R. Marshall)

136 (AVC 136)

Above: Walsgrave-on-Stowe is three miles north-east of Coventry, to the east of the River Stowe, and was for many years the terminus of the 6 bus route. Parked on the forecourt of the mock Jacobean-styled Red Lion Public House in Ansty Road, Walsgrave-on-Stowe, is Daimler COA6 136 (AVC 136). The COA6 model, with its AEC engine, could always be distinguished by the two access holes in the bonnet side. It is about 1949 and the Metro-Cammell bus body had, by now, been reseated to H27/26R, an increase of three on its original seating plan. Age did not help the looks of these MCCW bodies as they seemed to be stripped of any design fripperies and, coupled to the less elaborate post-war livery, began to look more gaunt. (D. R. Harvey Collection)

134 (AVC 134)

Opposite above: The Carl Rosa Operatic Company was playing at the Coventry Hippodrome theatre when Daimler COA6 134 (AVC 134) was parked outside. The opera company was founded in 1873 by Carl August Rosa, a German music impresario whose aim was to present German, French and Italian opera sung in English by well-known opera stars leading a company of new artistes. They toured the country going to theatres not usually known for putting on operatic productions and, with an aim to get the public interested, always kept their ticket prices low. The early post-war livery on the Metro-Cammell bodywork of bus 134, does look extremely smart, with the cream-painted upper-saloon guttering just adding a touch of quality. The Coventry bus fleet was always well maintained, and even buses in their dotage retained their front hub caps and looked smartly turned out. If 134 was representative of the mid-1930s Coventry fleet then the Metro-Cammell-bodied Daimler CVA6 behind it, 62 (GKV 62), came to be one of the stalwarts of the 1950s and 1960s. (D. R. Harvey Collection)

136 (AVC 136)

Opposite below: In 1938, and still in its first flush of youth, 136 (AVC 136) has just arrived in Broadgate. The bus is a Daimler COA6, with a Brush H26/24R body that had entered service in November 1935. A Maudslay ML4A single-decker bus comes out of Cross Cheaping in front of the almost brand new Owen Owen department store, which occupied the triangular junction with the recently opened Trinity Street. 136 is about to be overtaken by a Bristol-registered Standard Ten and a Rover 12. (D. R. Harvey Collection)

138 (AVC 138)

Above: MCCW-bodied Daimler COA6 138 (AVC 138) is in Pool Meadow bus station in 1944. It is painted in the all-over grey livery as the maroon colour paint normally associated with the fleet ran out of stock and then became unavailable due to the wartime strictures. It is also noticeable that the bus is not carrying the Coventry Transport fleet name on the lower-saloon waist rail. The bus would be repainted immediately after the war ended and would remain in service until 1951. (W. J. Haynes)

143 (BDU 143)

Above: Three Leyland Cub IKPO2s, numbered 143–145, entered service in January 1936 for use on the Brownshill Green service. They replaced the two Dennis 30 cwt fourteen-seaters, but were still too small and only lasted until 1938 when the three of them were sold for further service. These buses had the Leyland 4.7-litre six-cylinder petrol engine, which was very smooth running. The attractive Brush bodies, enhanced by the rear wheel spats, were of a B20F layout. 143 (BDU 143) is in Pool Meadow bus station on service 10 in October 1936. (R. T. Wilson)

140 (AVC 140)

Opposite below: 140 (AVC 140), a 1935-vintage MCCW-bodied Daimler COA6, is parked in Harnall Lane garage yard alongside an unidentified Maudslay ML4A. As these single-deckers were taken out of service by 1938, and the penultimate bus on the right, 166 (BKV 166), entered service in February 1937, this dates this line-up to the summer of that Coronation year. 166 is painted in the new livery style with the front cab apron and the pillars and window surrounds painted maroon instead of cream.

The rest of the line-up next to the unidentified Daimler CP6, located next to 140, is 110 (KV 7110), another Brush-bodied Daimler CP6, and 154 (BWK 154), a 1936 Brush-bodied bus that had the indignity of being the first COA6 to be withdrawn in 1947. Next to it on the right is 136 (AVC 136), another of the same class as 140, and finally the almost-new 166. The last unidentifiable bus is a BKV-registered Brush-bodied COA6. (A. J. Owen)

144 (BDU 144)

Left: The 17 service from Pool Meadow bus station to Baginton went via Broadgate and Warwick Road to its outer terminus. It was taken over from an operator called S. A. Smith and first operated on 1 April 1936. This was a semi-rural service, but with the proposed development of the Baginton area afoot, the Corporation saw an opportunity to develop the bus services into this housing area. In 1936, the grass strip known as Coventry Airport opened nearby, becoming an RAF base during the Second World War. Parked at the terminus is Brush-bodied Leyland Cub 144 (BDU 144), with the typical diagonal destination lettering on the blind. (A. J. Owen)

148 (BWK 148)

Above: The rather rundown Coventry Hippodrome stands opposite the bus operating on the 5 route to Coundon in about 1948. 148 (BWK 148), a Daimler COA6 with a Brush H29/26R body, was delivered in September 1936 and had Clayton Dewandre heaters in the lower saloon. 148 was one of thirty-seven buses that were rebuilt between 1944 and 1946 with new front bulkheads prefabricated by Metro-Cammell. This work was done at Keresley Works and gave the bus another four years of service. Behind the bus in Hales Street is the old fire station, built in 1902. (D. R. Harvey Collection)

146 (BHP 146)

Opposite below: When Birmingham Corporation ordered an extra ten Daimler COG5 single-deckers, numbered 32–41 (BOL 32–41), from Metro-Cammell for delivery in February and March 1936, the Washwood Heath body manufacturer gave the contract number 113. When Coventry Transport ordered a solitary Metro-Cammell-bodied Daimler COG5 for delivery in March 1936, Metro-Cammell added an eleventh body to the BCT specification and gave it their contract number 114. This Birmingham look alike bus was numbered 146 (BHP 146) and is parked in Pool Meadow bus station in about 1947. It was Coventry Transport's first COG5 single decker, which they later standardised in the 1940s. 146 is about to leave on the service to Berkswell. It later became well-known for many years in the Birmingham area as a showman's caravan. (J. Cull)

149 (BWK 149)

Above: Standing outside Coventry Hippodrome is 149 (BWK 149), a Brush-bodied Daimler COA6 and was built in 1936. It has an AEC indirect injection A171F 7.57-litre engine. 149 is working on the 7 service to Allesley in about 1948. This was rebuilt with Metro-Cammell front bulkheads in about 1945 and was fitted with seats trimmed in the standard post-war green and red rexine. All the double-deck buses numbered from 147, the first one of the class, through to 205, were bodied by Brush, who supplied similar bus bodies to Derby and Wolverhampton corporations on Daimler COG5 chassis. (S. N. J. White)

153 (BWK 153)

Above: 153 (BWK 153) is working on the 9 route to Copswood, off Binley Road to the east of the city centre, in about 1950. It was renumbered 453 in February 1952 and withdrawn two months later, having been the last of the 147–161 batch with its original body to remain in service, albeit with new Metro-Cammell bulkheads that were fitted at the end of the Second World War. This Brush-bodied Daimler COA6 still retained the low mounted headlights. It was only in January 1949 that legislation was enacted to specify the height of headlights. Many operators, including Newcastle and Nottingham corporations, used this low arrangement as it was the opinion that they were more efficient in this spotlight position in times of fog and, even worse, smog, which was very common before the Clean Air Act. (D. R. Harvey Collection)

152 (BWK 152)

Opposite below: The registration plates of all fifteen BWK-registered Daimler COA6s were mounted horizontally below the windscreen underneath the characteristic ledge, whereas on other buses it was carried lower down on the cab apron or as a square plate with the three registration letters above the three numbers. The raised registration marks were made of an alloy of copper, zinc and nickel as this combination was very hard wearing and bright. It was sometimes known as 'German Silver'. When new, the fifteen 1936 buses had the luxury of having Clayton Dewandre heaters in the lower saloon, although these were taken out during the Second World War. 152 (BWK 152) is working on the 5 route to Coundon Road and is being followed by a 1939 Warwickshire-registered Standard Flying Eight. (S. L. Poole)

155 (BWK 155)

Above: Loading up with passengers in Broadgate on New Year's Eve in 1948 is 155 (BWK 155), a 1936 Brush-bodied Daimler COA6. It is working on the 9 route to Earlsdon about one mile to the west of the city centre. Just visible behind the bus is part of the thirteenth-century Holy Trinity church. 155 was the first of five COA6s to be rebodied by Roe in April 1949. About to overtake 155 is as-use unrebuilt wartime 342 (EKV 942), a Daimler CWA6 with a Weymann UH30/26R body working to Coventry railway station. (A. A. Cooper)

160 (BWK 160)

Above: For some reason lost in the mists of time, the Brush H29/26R on 160 (BWK 160) was fitted with flared lower-body panels that considerably altered the appearance of the bus. Save for this strange body anomaly, 160 was a standard Daimler COA6. This outward curving of the lower body panels was usually more associated with bodies constructed by Weymann and actually suited the body design specified by Coventry Transport extremely well. The bus is parked on Earl Street just beyond the Council House in front of the Herbert Art Gallery and Museum site when working on the 1 route. (D. R. Harvey Collection)

155 (BWK 155)

Opposite below: After rebodying with an attractive new Roe H31/26R body, 155 (BWK 155) looked like a new bus as even the chassis had been renovated. This was one of five COA6s rebodied by Roe, with the others being 161, 173, 199 and 201. Charles Roe, not one of the coachbuilders usually favoured by West Midlands-based municipalities, also got a contract to rebody all twenty of Wolverhampton Corporation Guy Arab IIs in 1950 and 1951 with similarly styled bodywork. 155 is on delivery to Coventry in April 1949 and is carrying trade plate 266 RW. (D. R. Harvey Collection)

164 (BKV 164)

Above: 164 (BKV 164), was one of the 1937 deliveries of twelve more Brush-bodied Daimler COA6. 164 was rebodied in 1942 after most of its original body was destroyed by air-raid damage with a new Brush sixty-seat body. The top deck went onto 109 (KV 7109), a Daimler CP6, in 1942. Like 252 of 1940, which was the first body to have the redesigned bodies that had curved, upswept, radiused, end-saloon windows, 164 was fitted with this new style of body when it was rebodied by Brush along with six others in 1942. It is working on the 11 route and is parked outside George Wigglestone's shop. Despite its new body, 164 was withdrawn in 1949. (R. Marshall)

168 (BKV 168)

Above: Despite all the restrictions and lack of materials during the early part of the Second World War, Coventry Transport generally managed to keep their bus fleet in good condition. 168 (BKV 168), although equipped with headlight masks, tinted blackout windows and white edging paint, looks in remarkably fine fettle as it works towards Pool Meadow bus station in the city centre. All headlight masks were removed from Coventry's fleet in January 1945, when the threat of bombing raids was declared over. This was one of the last six of the batch which were fitted with direct injection AEC A173 7.57-litre engines from new. (S. L. Poole)

167 (CWK 167)

Opposite below: 167 (CWK 167) was barely nine months old when it stood in Broadgate on 7 October 1937. It is working on the Earlsdon service. Behind the bus are the early fifteenth-century half-timbered Lychgate Cottages, while to the left is the open, but still incomplete, Trinity Street, which was opened earlier in 1937. The buses introduced a new livery variation with the saloon pillars painted maroon rather than cream. These Daimler COA6s, with Brush H29/26R bodywork, were fitted with Clayton Dewandre heaters in the upper saloon. This bus was totally destroyed in an air raid on 8 April 1941. (J. S. Webb)

171 (BKV 171)

The driver reads his newspaper at the terminus of the 5 route at Coundon in January 1952 before setting out for the terminus at the Hippodrome. His charge is 171 (BKV 171), one of the 1937 Brush-bodied Daimler COA6s that had received new pillars and a new lower-saloon front bulkhead in around 1945. These buses were the first in the fleet to have the square two-line number plate mounted on the front cab panel, which was the only panel supplied by the chassis builder. Despite being retrimmed in the new post-war green and red rexine in 1949, 171 was taken out of service in 1952 and was sold to Birds, the well-known Stratford scrap dealer, in February 1952 and promptly broken up. (A. A. Cooper)

174 (AMV 433)

A mid-blue and cream painted AEC Q-type demonstrator, AMV 433, was on long-term hire to Coventry from 1937 until January 1938, although it did also briefly appear in Coventry in 1934. This was an oil-engined vehicle and had the engine mounted between the wheelbase on the offside of the chassis, which enabled the bodywork to have an entrance ahead of the front axle. The Q was revolutionary and thus did not catch on, with only twenty-three double-deck motorbuses being constructed. AMV 433 had a Park Royal H31/29F bodywork, weighing 5 tons, 19 ½ cwt, mounted on chassis O761016 and was the last of the five AEC Q demonstrator to be constructed. This was the first AEC Q double-decker to have a folding door into the lower saloon from the open front platform as previous vehicles were notorious for draughts. It was used mainly on the Inner Circle 14 service and was reputedly given the fleet number 174. AMV 433 was the only one of the Q demonstrators not to be sold, and was demonstrated to Nottingham, Cardiff and Coventry corporations over a four-year period, ending when it was returned to AEC from Coventry at the end of its demonstration period. It was broken up at the end of 1938. (R. T. Wilson)

JR 1573

Above: Completed as a demonstrator for Transport Vehicles (Daimler) in February 1934, JR 1573 was only the second Daimler COG5 to be built. It was fitted with a Weymann H24/24R composite-construction body registered in Northumberland. It was on loan to Coventry from May 1937 until it was returned to Daimler during February 1938 and operated in the full maroon and cream livery. It is crossing from Smithford Street into High Street in 1937, with the art deco-styled Burton's tailors shop on the corner of the south end of Broadgate behind it, when working on the 4 service to Stoke Heath. (Commercial Postcard)

176 (CWK 176)

Above: It was a strange quirk of policy that resulted in all but one of the Daimler COG5 single-deckers being bodied by Park Royal, whereas the double-deck orders were almost exclusively split between Brush and Metro-Cammell, with the exception of the solitary Massey-bodied example and the three Park Royal-bodied buses of 1938. 176 (CWK 176) was the third member of the quintet of Daimler COG5/40 single-deckers and was the first to be painted in the standard fleet livery of maroon with cream waist rails. These buses had both their side destination boxes mounted at the top of a window bay at the rear of the bus. It is working on the Burton Green service near to Hearsall Green not long after its delivery in January 1938. (A. J. Owen)

174 (CWK 174)

Opposite below: Parked in Wheatley Street alongside the old mill is 174 (CWK 174). The first two of these Park Royal B38F-bodied Daimler COG5/40s were painted in a reversed all-over cream livery with a maroon side flash for use on private hire services. 174 entered service in December 1937. They were fitted with luxurious seating almost up to coach standards. The Outer Circle 19 route was reintroduced in May 1948, having originally been instigated in 1938. It was a 30-mile-long route and was promoted as a sightseeing tour of the city boundary with the instructions to 'See the New Housing Estates and Development Schemes – Great Industries – Places of Historical Interest and Lovely Panoramic Views.' All five of these buses were taken out of service in 1949 when they were replaced in that year by Brush-bodied Daimler CVD6s. (A.Ingram)

185 (CWK 185)

Above: Daimler COA6 185 (CWK 185) is parked in the bus lay-by outside the Herbert Library Art Gallery in Jordan Well when working on the 11 route. Behind the bus is the Council House, built during the First World War. The bus is a 1938 Brush-bodied Daimler COA6. The Brush bodies were not as robust as the Metro-Cammell-bodied examples and 185 was one of many that received new MCCW bulkheads and body pillars in order to extend their lives. In this case, 185 survived until 1951. (D. R. Harvey Collection)

179 (CWK179)

Opposite above: Entering service in December 1937, 179 (CWK 179) was the first of three Park Royal-bodied Daimler COA6s. The metal-framed buses were constructed to Mr Fearnley's exacting standards and were virtually indistinguishable from the bodies being constructed by Brush. These were the first class of buses to receive from new the legend 'COVENTRY TRANSPORT' on the lower-saloon waist rail, but the experiments with saloon heaters was finally abandoned. They were also the last buses to have maroon as the main interior colour for the leather and moquette seating and trim; the next and subsequent deliveries changed to green as the new saloon colour. 179 is parked at the Binley terminus of the 5 route in about 1941. The saloon windows are covered with blue lacquer blackout masking to prevent the reduced interior lighting from being seen at night. (S. L. Poole)

181 (CWK 181)

Opposite below: The last of the trio of Park Royal-bodied Daimler COA6s was 181 (CWK 181). This bus was not withdrawn until January 1952, thus becoming the last of the three to remain in service. It even had its seats and interior retrimmed in the standard post-war green and red rexine. Near to the end of its life, with some dents around the bottom of the cab and buckling panels on the panels between the decks, 181 is parked at Poole Meadow bus station when being used on the 6 route to Wyken from Coventry railway station. (J. Cull)

186 (CWK186)

A well-laden 186 (CWK186), a 1938 Brush H29/26R-bodied Daimler COA6 unloads passengers on their way into the city at the Utility bus shelters outside Coventry Hippodrome. The bus has still got its blackout regulation white edgings to the front mudguards, but the headlight masks have been removed, so it must be in the spring of 1945. The art deco design of the 2,000-seater New Hippodrome, which opened on 1 November 1937, was an easily recognisable landmark in Hales Street, even when it became The Coventry Theatre and, later, The Apollo. It closed as a theatre in 1985 and was demolished in 2002 to make way for the Coventry Transport Museum and Millennium Place, Hales Street. (W. J. Haynes)

186 (CWK 186)

Contrasting with the post-war 26 (FHP 26), a Daimler CVA6 that had entered service in September 1948, is 186 (CWK 186), a Brush-bodied Daimler COA6 dating from January 1938. They are both well-laden with workers when working on the 16A along Keresley Road and 16 routes respectively. Neither bus is wearing advertisements, but whereas the body panels on the still quite new 26 are pristine, those on 186 are heavily rippled, suggesting that all was not well with the body pillars despite the bus being one of sixteen of the 182–205 class to be rebuilt with Metro-Cammell bulkheads and body pillars. (R. Wilson)

187 (CWK 187)
Parked on Earl Street, just beyond the 1920s-built Council House and in front of the Herbert Art Gallery Museum while working on the 1A route, is Brush-bodied Daimler COA6 187 (CWK 187). Soaring above the bus in the distance is the early fifteenth-century perpendicular tower of Coventry Cathedral, which was the only part of St Michael's church to survive the bombing of Coventry on the night of 14 November 1940. 187 was rebuilt with Metro-Cammell body pillars and bulkheads in about 1945, and its interior was retrimmed with the standard post-war green and red rexine. All this work was obviously a worthwhile investment in this case, as 187 was one of only thirteen COA6s to survive to 1956 and the only one to be renumbered into the duplicate list as 487. (D. R. Harvey Collection)

191 (CWK 191)
Parked alongside the temporary shops in Broadgate in 1953, the same year as it was withdrawn, is 191 (CWK 191), a Brush-bodied Daimler COA6 dating from January 1938 with a H29/26R seating layout. It is working on the 16A route to Keresley Village. These 182–205 class buses represented the ultimate in the first style of bodies built to Ronald Fearnley's specification. Built originally with AEC A171RB engines, they were gradually converted to the more efficient A173 7.57-litre direct injection engines. The conductress poses by the nearside front wing before getting onto the bus to collect the fares from the already seated passengers. (P. Tizard)

195 (CWK 195)

Above: The timber-frame jettied frontage and large bay windows looked medieval, but were actually built in 1938 to blend in with the genuine medieval buildings behind it. For many years these were the premises of Timothy Whites, the chemist whose shop is visible behind 195 (CWK 195), a Brush-bodied Daimler COA6 also built in 1938. The bus is parked at the top of Trinity Street at the entrance to Broadgate. The empty bus is about to return to Harnall Lane garage. The front profile of Coventry's buses of this vintage always looked very severe; this was due to the heavy built-in cab sun visor, the shallow-angled windscreen and the bulging ledge above the cab apron, resulting in the front profile being broken. (R. Marshall)

199 (CWK 199)

Above: In May 1949, five of the 1936 and 1937 Daimler COA6s were overhauled, reconditioned and fitted with new Charles Roe ash-framed H31/26R bodies. Another twelve of the war-time Daimler CWA6s were similarly rebodied two years later. 199 (CWK 199) was one of the COA6s to be rebodied with their attractive deep-windowed body design. They had typical rebody features including the Roe patent staircase, the curved staircase window and the teak waist rail moulding. It is standing in Pool Meadow bus station in 1950 when working on the 10 route to Brownshill Green. Parked behind 199 is Coventry's 330 (EKV 930), their only lowbridge bus. (J. Cockshott)

196 (CWK 196)

Opposite below: The temporary shops in Broadgate were opened in about 1947 and, amazingly, remained in use until 1974. Parked outside them when working on the 2 route is another of the 1937/38 delivered batch of twenty-four Brush-bodied Daimler COA6s. These entered service with AEC A171RB indirect injection 7.57-litre oil engines. They were all converted to the new A173 engine in 1939 in an attempt to improve fuel economy. The A173, introduced in 1936 but not publicised until July 1938, was AEC's first direct-injection oil engine. 196 survived until 1956, having been rebuilt with Metro-Cammell bulkheads and body pillars in 1945 and having its interior retrimmed with the standard post-war rexine colours. (R. H. G. Simpson)

201 (CWK 201)

Above: Coventry Transport rebodied five Daimler COA6s in April 1949, including 201 (CWK 201), all with Charles Roe H31/26R bodywork. It stands in Broadgate in the early 1950s when working on the 21 route. The rebodied bus, at first sight, appeared to be a new bus, like the 1949 bus 55 (GKV 55), a Daimler CVA6 with an MCCW sixty-seater body, parked behind 201. The rebodied COA6 would remain in service with Coventry until 1958, having been renumbered two years earlier. Even then it ran for another four years as a mobile furniture showroom. (R. A. Mills)

201 (CWK 201)

Opposite: With its roof covered in camouflage paint, 201 (CWK 201), with its original body, is working on the 9 route between Earlsdon and Lower Stoke. It was introduced in November 1941 to replace the discontinued tram route. The crew pose in front of the Brush-bodied Daimler COA6 in its original condition at the Earlsdon terminus early in 1942. The bus still has all the wartime blackout additions and would continue in this form until rebodied by Charles Roe in 1949. (A. J. Owen)

202 (CWK 202)

Above: The crew and the traffic inspector pose in front of their charge, 202 (CWK 202), as it stands at the terminus of the 11A route at Hartington Crescent, Earlsdon, some 200 yards beyond the former terminus of the Earlsdon leg of the 8 tram service. Drivers and conductors dreaded the sight of the military capped inspectors who were checking for drivers running early, running late, smoking on duty, complaints about driving and the conductors' waybill, the issuing of the correct tickets and the collection of fares. The 11A route ran from Pool Meadow via Trinity Street, Broadgate, Hertford Street, Warwick Road, The Butts, Radcliffe Road and Beechwood Avenue. The bus is a Daimler COA6 and is almost brand new, being still fitted with the built-in sun visor over the cab windscreen and a highly polished nutguard ring on the offside front wheel which also served as an extra step for the driver to use in order into the cab. (A. J. Owen)

205 (CWK 205)

Opposite above: The last of the CWK-registered Daimler COA6s entered service on 9 April 1938 and was equipped with chassis automatic lubrication. The delivery of 205 (CWK 205) was delayed by the body being specified with an all-over cream livery with maroon window surrounds, roof and waist rail bands. It was obviously nicknamed *The White Lady*. It was also something of a 'pet' bus and as such survived until December 1955, by which time it had achieved 657,039 miles. It ran concurrently with 100 (GKV 100), which entered service in 1951 as the post-war reverse-livery double-decker for some four years. 205 stands at the Trinity Street end of Broadgate when working on the 9 route to Earlsdon after advertisements were introduce to the bus fleet in 1951. (D. R. Harvey Collection)

203 (CWK 203)

Above: Coventry Transport had one of their prized new buses exhibited at the November 1937 Commercial Motor Show at Olympia. Daimler COA6 203 (CWK 203) had a Brush H29/26R body finished to a highly polished standard. The radiator was chromed to a superior finish and the pair of access holes on the bonnet side were also chromed. 203 has just returned from the show in December 1937 and is parked outside the Harnall Lane garage with the destination blind for the intended 20 route, which would have been the Bedworth tram replacement bus service scheduled for closure during 1940. The tram route was reprieved in 1939 because of the worsening international situation, but was precipitately replaced by buses after the bombing of 14/15 November 1940. (D. R. Harvey Collection)

206 (DHP 206)

Above: In April 1938 three more Park Royal-bodied Daimler COG5/40s were delivered and although they had bus seats, they were a rather luxurious green and rust colour. These three had a rear-mounted offside destination box, whereas the next three COG5/40s delivered a few months later had the offside destination box located at the front of the body. 206 (DHP 206) is parked in Pool Meadow bus station in 1943, and the lack of a shiny roof suggests that it is painted grey. (W. J. Haynes)

208 (DHP 208)

Opposite Above: Waiting at the bus stop at the Trinity Street end of Broadgate on a hot summer's day, with all its saloon ventilator windows wide open, is 208 (DHP 208), the last of the first three DHP-registered Park Royal-bodied Daimler COG5/40s that entered service in April 1938. This bus was the only one of the batch to be converted to a B32F layout, with perimeter seating, in July 1942, and was returned to its original seating layout of B38F, in this case in December 1945. Behind the bus and through the trees in Priory Row is the fifteenth-century half-timbered row of Lychgate Cottages. Parked behind 208 is 243 (EVC 243), another Daimler COG5/40 with a Park Royal B38F body that had entered service in May 1940. (A. A. Cooper)

211 (DWK 211)

Opposite below: Coventry Transport ordered four batches of three Daimler COG5/40 single-deckers; the CWK-registered buses for delivery in 1937, two groups of three in 1938 and the EVC-registered ones in 1940. 211 (DWK 211) was the last of the three to enter service in June 1938. These had their offside destination boxes mounted at the front of the saloon in the cant rail. As with all the other COG5/40 single-deckers, 211 was taken out of service in 1949 and sold to Yeoman's of Canon Pyon in Herefordshire, who ran it for two years. It was then operated as a showman's vehicle and a caravan and storage vehicle, being used on the fairground scene until the late 1950s. It is standing in Lightwoods Park in Bearwood with its owner standing in the roof-mounted cargo container. (D. Williams)

212 (DKV 212)

On 15 April 1954, Wilfred Pickles was appearing in the play *The Gay Dog*, written by Joseph Cotton, at Coventry Hippodrome. Parked outside on Hales Street is the first of the Metro-Cammell H30/26R-bodied Daimler COA6s, 212 (DKV 212), which entered service in March 1939. It is waiting to go to Highfield Road on a Coventry City football special. This was the first of eleven buses that began a slight alteration in the ordering policy, with a movement away from exclusively having bodies produced by Brush of Loughborough. Gone was the built-in sun visor over the windscreen, while the saloon windows had radiused bottom edges. The cab arrangement was inherited from designs produced for Birmingham, Edinburgh and West Bromwich corporations and was a lot neater than those on the corresponding Brush bodies. The Metro-Cammell bodies also had the roof framework mounted externally, giving a very purposeful look. Also working on a football service behind it is Brush-bodied Daimler COA6 192 (CWK 192). (R. Marshall)

213 (DKV 213)

Parked in Broadgate, outside the temporary shops in front of Trinity church, is 213 (DKV 213), a Daimler COA6 with a Metro-Cammell H30/26R body that was fitted from new with the AEC A173 direct injection 7.57-litre engine. It is working on the 16 route to Green Lane in about 1950. When new, these eleven buses operated with an H29/26R layout, but after about a week all the vehicles were quickly reseated. In 1954, 213 received seats from three of the 1949 Brush-bodied Daimler CVD6s. With the addition of the Massey-bodied 223 (DKV 223), these were the only fifty-six-seater Daimler-built buses in the pre-war fleet. (W. J. Haynes)

214 (DKV 214)

Above: Parked at the 8A bus shelter in Pool Meadow bus station in 1945 is 214 (DKV 214). This MCCW-bodied Daimler COA6 is working to Tile Hill North. Surprisingly, the bus still has the remnants of gold lining out on the front cab panel. It seemed to be the normal mode of operation that when a bus arrived at a city centre terminal, including Pool Meadow, the bus driver left the cab as opposed to the more normal practice of waiting in the cab with the engine running for the departure time. (J. Cull)

216 (DKV 216)

Above: Operating on the 20 route over the cobbled road surface and the remnants of the abandoned tram tracks is 216 (DKV 216). It is working from Bedworth via Foleshill to the railway station on 14 May 1944. This Metro-Cammell-bodied Daimler COA6 is still wearing headlight masks and, after the privations of the Second World War, its paintwork looks in dire need of refreshing. One wartime economic alteration was the removal of the upper-saloon side destination blinds, which were never replaced after hostilities ended. (J. Cull)

215 (DKV 215)

Opposite below: Working on the 21 route to Bell Green via Stoney Stanton Road, Bell Green Road and Alderman's Green Road and Lenton's Lane is 215 (DKV 215), a Metro-Cammell-bodied Daimler COA6. For some reason the half-drop saloon windows appear to have been recently rechromed. Delivered in April 1939, all that year's deliveries of COA6s were equipped from new with the direct injection AEC A173 and after just one week in service all the batch received an extra upper saloon seat, thus becoming H30/26R. The previously standard built-in sun visor was omitted for the first time with these buses, which considerably tidied up the bus front profile. (R. A. Mills)

217 (DKV 217)

About to leave the Tile Hill terminus on the 8 route is 217 (DKV 217). The efficient conductor of this Daimler COA6 has already wound round its front destination blind for its return journey to Pool Meadow bus station. The bus still sports headlights in the low position that would be made illegal by the mid-1950s. The single oil filler access hole on the bonnet side was always the identifying feature of these AEC-engined COA6s. This bus had a Metro-Cammell H30/26R body, but was unfortunately one of five of the 212–222 classes that were badly damaged in the 14 November air raid and subsequently fitted with a new Brush roof in 1941. In this form it lasted until 1955. (D. R. Harvey Collection)

218 (DKV 218)

218 (DKV 218), a Daimler COA6 with a MCCW H30/26R body, was virtually new when working on the 11A service to Earlsdon. It is passing the Quadrant at the north end of Greyfriars Green during early 1939. The ribbed, full-length, nearside front wing was a design unique to Coventry's pre-war COA6 model. The bus was to survive the war without damage, and it was a testament to the strength of the metal-framed construction by Metro-Cammell that 218 lasted until 1956 with little alteration. (W. J. Haynes)

219 (DKV 219)

Above: A little girl and, a few seats further back, a slightly dour-looking man watch Jack White with curiosity as he takes the photograph of 219 (DKV 219), looking a little battered around the rear mudguard, as it lies over when working on the 13 service to Willenhall. This Metro-Cammell-bodied Daimler COA6 was one of three in the class of eleven that were badly damaged in November 1940 and subsequently received new roofs supplied by Brush. These roofs were deeper than the Metro-Cammell ones they replaced and did not have external framework, giving a much smoother profile. (S. N. J. White)

220 (DKV 220)

Left: Although a rather poor photograph, bus 220 (DKV 220) shows off in some detail the all-over wartime grey livery. The cream areas are painted over, leaving only the beading as a reminder of where it used to be. The life rail and the bottom of the rear platform panel have been painted white in order to show other road users where the edges of the bus were during the blackout. The bus, a Metro-Cammell-bodied Daimler COA6, is about to work on the Keresley service after its driver and conductress have finished posing for the photographer. (D. R. Harvey Collection)

221 (DKV 221)

Prior to being delivered in May 1939, 221 (DKV 221) was chosen by bodybuilder Metro-Cammell to be photographed as the official representative of the 212–222 classes of eleven buses. Although equipped with standard Coventry Transport specification fixtures and fittings, the bodywork was basically the standard product built by the Birmingham-based company. This body style was built for Edinburgh, Newcastle and West Bromwich corporations but the Coventry examples did have the luxury of radiuses to the bottom corners of the saloon windows. These metal-framed bodies were generally more robust than the contemporary Coventry Transport Brush-bodied Daimler COA6s and 221 survived until 1956 without any major reconstruction work. (MCCW)

222 (DKV 222)

After withdrawal, most pre-war Coventry double-deckers were sold to various dealers for scrap and only a few escaped to be operated by other operators. 222 (DKV 222) was sold to R. Irvine (t/a Tiger Coaches), acting as a dealer, in August 1953 before being sold in February 1955 to Cunningham's Bus Service of Paisley. Although fully repainted in Cunningham's green livery, this extremely smart-looking Daimler COA6 only lasted in service until September 1956 when it was withdrawn and promptly scrapped. (D. R. Harvey Collection)

225 (DKV 225)

Left: The terminus of the 6 bus route in Ansty Road, Walsgrave-on-Stowe, was on the forecourt of the Jacobean-styled Red Lion public house. Bus 225 (DKV 225), a Brush-bodied Daimler COA6, had entered service in March 1939 but by the early 1950s the bus had the look of a bus which had seen better days. Much of the chrome work had been painted over and the cab apron had acquired the battle scars of many minor confrontations. The cab apron, where the number plate was located, was part of the chassis structure while the area below the angled windscreen was part of the body. This enabled the cab area to 'float' and the gap between the cab area and the cab apron was sealed against draughts by a concealed thick rubber strip. (D. R. Harvey Collection)

223 (DKV223)

Above: It usually took several months between a bus being withdrawn and then being disposed of to a dealer, scrap merchant or even for resale. 223 (DKV 223), the unique Massey-bodied Daimler COA6, was withdrawn in 1953 but was dumped at the rear of Keresley Works before being sold to Belgrave Autos, Mitcham in 1956. The shabby-looking bus is in stark contrast to the smart vehicle that was proudly posed outside Massey's factory as their first metal-framed bus body in the summer of 1939. Also dumped and awaiting their fate are the severely accident-damaged 228 (DKV 228), a Daimler COG5/60 with a Brush body, and 200 (CWK 200), another Daimler COA6 with Brush bodywork. Both 200 and 228 were sold to Remblance, who was a London dealer in buses. (A. D. Broughall)

223 (DKV 223)

Opposite above: The first ever Massey Brothers metal-framed body was completed in June 1939 as Coventry 223 (DKV 223), a Daimler COA6 with fifty-six seats. This one-off body could easily be distinguished by the deep-angled lower profile windscreen that carried on the profile of the upper saloon. The chassis was one of a batch of eighteen, Nos 212–222 carrying Metro-Cammell bodies and Nos 224–229 carrying Brush bodies. The single Massey body was bought for comparative purposes.

The Transport Committee placed the order in July 1938 and whereas the tender received for the Brush Electrical Engineering Co. Ltd was £1,018, and that for the Metro-Cammell Ltd bodies was for £1,021 per body, the tender for the solitary Massey Bros (Wigan) body was just £890. It appears that Massey seriously underestimated the true cost of production and went back to composite construction until 1950, when they built their next metal-framed bus for Birkenhead Corporation. The body was rebuilt in 1946 and the bus withdrawn in 1953. It is parked at the 11 route terminus at The Bull's Head public house. (R. Marshall)

226 (DKV 226)

Above: Standing in the Broadgate area, while it was being reconstructed in about 1952, is one of the six Brush H29/26R-bodied Daimler COA6s delivered during March 1939. 226 (DKV 226) was rebuilt by CCT at Keresley Works during July 1946 rather than receiving MCCW bulkheads, which was the case for four of the class. They must have done a good job as 226 remained in service until 1956. Advertisements were introduce to the bus fleet in 1951, 226 began carrying one for Marston's Burton Bitter. This bus was also one of a small number of vehicles to have the fleet number moved onto the waist rail. This new experimental position was not pursued, which was a shame as it did look better than the usual position on the top of the front lower-saloon panels. (D. R. Harvey Collection)

227 (DKV 227)

Opposite above: The angled windscreen on 227 (DKV 227), a 1939 Brush-bodied Daimler COA6, is clearly visible as it stands in Pool Meadow bus station when working on the 8 route to Tile Hill. This feature, though aesthetically unpleasant, was a deliberately specified feature designed to eliminate reflections from the illuminated lower saloon at night. These bodies were of a new design, having a more modern curved front profile. 227 had not long emerged from Keresley Works, where it had received new MCCW bulkheads in a fairly extensive rebuilding programme ending in 1949. This affected some thirty-six of the late 1930s Brush bodies. (S. N. J. White)

228 (DKV 228)

Opposite below: Already well loaded up with passengers in Pool Meadow bus station is Daimler COA6 228 (DKV 228). From this angle, the well-rounded bodywork produced by Brush becomes more evident. This was similar to nearby Birmingham, where dual sourcing of bus bodies involved the purchasing of Metro-Cammell and Birmingham Railway & Carriage Co. bodies. The latter proved to be distinctly frailer, so there was a parallel to Coventry. Here, again, Metro-Cammell bodies were latterly specified in the late 1930s, while Brush bodies were ordered almost exclusively until 1937, and many of them required rebuilding. This included 228, which was fitted with MCCW bulkheads in about 1948. (D. R. Harvey Collection)

230 (EHP 230)

Left: Delivered at the end of July 1939 was 230 (EHP 230), Daimler COG5/60s. There were nine of these chassis delivered in 1939 and the first four were numbered 230 to 233. Another twelve arrived in the summer and autumn of 1940 and were only supplied to Coventry Transport. The metal-framed Brush bodywork squeezed in thirty-one passengers in the lower saloon, twenty-nine upstairs and was another new Brush body design. The upper-saloon bulkhead pillars were much thicker, giving more rigidity to the structure and precluding the need for replacement bulkheads after around seven years service. They were the first 26-foot-long double-deckers on two axles to be built with a total seating capacity of sixty passengers. 230 is parked at the 16A terminus at Keresley when almost new. (A. J. Owen)

231 (EHP 231)

Above: 231 (EHP 231) stands at the Radford terminus of the 2 route with the driver and conductor standing at the front of their bus. It is near to the art deco Cheylesmore public house on Daventry Road in the early weeks of the Second World War, not long after it was delivered in August 1939. Although still brand new, the bus has a grey camouflaged roof and has headlight masks and white edging paint on the mudguards. The bus is a Daimler COG5/60 with a sixty-seater Brush body and was delivered to Coventry Transport in August 1939. Normal COG5s had sloping radiators, but the COG5/60 model had a vertical radiator that allowed a few inches to be added to the lower saloon as part of the redesign, which enabled the lower-saloon front bulkhead to be moved forward. This meant that the bodied vehicle could seat sixty passengers. (A. J. Owen)

229 (DKV 229)

Opposite above: The Brush bodies delivered after 1939 had a more curved front profile than the earlier buses, which gave the buses a less severe and more modern appearance. 229 (DKV 229), a 1939 Daimler COA6, stands at the top of Trinity Street at the edge of Broadgate. This was the last pre-war bus to be delivered with a seating capacity of fifty-six passengers. After this all buses were built to carry sixty seated passengers. Behind bus 229, beyond the flower beds, is Priory Row with the fifteenth-century, half-timbered row of Lychgate Cottages. The bus is bound for Coventry railway station when working on the 20 service from Bedworth. Every third bus on this service was extended from Broadgate to the railway station. The bus was to remain in service until 1953 and although it was sold to Irvine of Salsburgh in August of that year, it was not sold on and was fairly quickly broken up. (D. R. Harvey Collection)

232 (EHP 232)

Above left: Standing in Harnall Lane garage yard in about 1941 and wearing the full wartime blackout regulations is 232 (EHP 232), the last of the quartet of the first of Coventry's new Daimler COG5/60 model. The COG5/60 had a very compact bonnet and engine compartment and had a vertical radiator which, within the strict limits of the 26-foot-long Construction & Use Regulations, enabled the lower saloon to accommodate thirty-one passengers downstairs. Only twenty-one COG5/60s were built before the cessation of pre-war model bus chassis production at the end of 1940 and all were supplied to Coventry Transport with Brush H29/31R bodies. (A. J. Owen)

234 (EHP 234)

Below left: The Earlsdon terminus of the 9 route went across the city centre to terminate at Gosford Green on Binley Road, taking over from the withdrawn trams on the 8 route when the bombings of the night of 14/15 November 1940 closed the tram system. Lightweight sixty-seater Metro-Cammell-bodied Daimler COA6 234 (EHP 234) is at the Earlsdon terminus of the 9 service in the spring of 1940 during the period of the Phoney War, prior to the evacuation of Allied soldiers from the beaches and harbour of Dunkirk, France, between 27 May and 4 June 1940. This terminus was located in Beechwood Avenue at Hartington Crescent. Passengers got off their bus just before the bend in Beechwood Avenue, after which the bus turned round in the throat of Hartington Crescent and waited to pick up passengers for the inbound journey. (A. J. Owen)

235 (EHP 235)

Above right: As an early post-war
Jaguar 1 ½-litre saloon disappears into
St Mary's Street, with the Council House
on Earl Street behind it, 235 (EHP 235),
a 1939 Metro-Cammell H31/29R-bodied
Daimler COA6 is parked in the bus lay-by
in Jordan Well. Along the bus is the site
for the Herbert Library Art Gallery. This
was named after Sir Alfred Herbert, the
Coventry industrialist and philanthropist
whose gift to the City allowed
construction to begin in 1939. Due to the
damage to Coventry in the Second World
War, and the need to rebuild the central
area, the original building was eventually
opened in 1960. 235 (EHP 235) is
working on the 11 route to Binley.
(D. R. Harvey Collection)

236 (EHP 236)

Below right: The variations in the
liveries of Coventry buses were subject
to minor tweaks on an experimental
basis from the late 1930s until the late
1940s, though obviously some of this
was due to having supplies of suitably
coloured paint. 236 (EHP 236), a Daimler
COA6, was delivered to Coventry
in December 1939 as part of the
four bodies built by Metro-Cammell
as part of their 221 contract. They
had lightweight construction bodies
weighing less than 6 ½ tons, and they
had continuous vertical panels between
the lower and upper deck windows in
order to further lighten the bus. By about
1952 it had been repainted with cream
window surrounds, while the waist
rail and all the side panelling above the
lower-saloon windows were painted
maroon. These four bodies constructed
by Metro-Cammell were their first foray
into lightweight construction, and many
of the lessons learnt with these units were
utilised in mass production when the
lightweight Orion body was developed
in 1954. The bus is in Pool Meadow bus
station and is working on the 8 route to
Bell Green. 236 survived in service until
1956. (A. D. Broughall)

239 (EWK 239)

Above: All twenty-one of Coventry's Daimler COG5/60s were bodied by Brush and whereas the seating layout on the Metro-Cammell-bodied COA6 chassis was H31/29R, on the Gardner 5LW-engined buses the seating layout was reversed, with thirty-one passengers in the lower saloon. This was arranged in this format in order for the bus to pass the tilt test regulations. The complete bus weighed under 5 ½ tons, but although the seat frames were light, the seating itself was extremely comfortable. This official Brush photograph of 239 (EWK 239), dating from November 1939, shows the bus in full blackout garb even to the extent of having the windows masked with blue lacquer. (Brush)

240 (EWK 240)

Above: Parked on the Harnall Lane garage forecourt in about 1950 is the rebodied 240 (EWK 240). The bus has the briefly used waist rail mounted fleet number. Actually written off along with 122 and 183 after the bombing raids of the night of 14/15 November 1940, 240 was reprieved and reentered service in November 1942. It was fitted with a quite early MoS specification body, built by Brush. The seating was of the standard pre-war Coventry type but it was arranged in an H31/29R 1939 layout. The early wartime Brush bodies could always be easily recognised by their square front upper-saloon side windows. In April 1945, 240 was fitted with the new Daimler CD6 8.6-litre engine for in-service testing. 253, 256 and 257 also followed soon afterwards, retaining the Daimler engine until they were withdrawn. 240 would stay in service until 1955, and even then was sold for further service with Irvine of Salsburgh. (D. R. Harvey Collection)

240 (EWK 240)

Opposite below: On 15 November 1940, bus 240 (EWK 240), a Brush-bodied Daimler COG5/60 delivered in December 1940, was apparently written-off when it was caught in the infamous air raid that began at 7.10 p.m. and didn't finish until 6.15 a.m. the following morning, by which time there were almost 600 dead and 2,306 houses that were destroyed or required demolition. It was about to depart for Keresley from the top of Cross Cheaping when its body was reduced to a twisted, mangled wreck. Amazingly, the chassis was salvaged, rebuilt and rebodied when it was discovered that there was enough of the chassis to warrant rebuilding. (D. R. Harvey Collection)

4 (CP 8010)

Due to the late delivery of new buses, four petrol-engined AEC Regent 661 double-deckers arrived on hire in December 1938 from AEC. Two of them, numbered 4 and 5 in the Coventry fleet, had been Halifax Corporation 54 and 55, while 1 and 7 had been in the Halifax JOC fleet as their 114 and 107. 4 (CP 8010) was initially operated in Coventry in its original green and orange Halifax livery and dated from 1929. The body was built by Hoyal and had an outside staircase-bodied H26/24R layout with a 'camel' roof which had a raised centre section over the upper-saloon gangway, to AEC-design, that gave the impression of a low-build body. They had crash gearboxes and were not popular with drivers and were therefore restricted to part-day operation.

Coventry livery was applied in the summer of 1939 and it was purchased in April 1940 for £25. 4 stands outside Holy Trinity church at the top of Trinity Street in July 1939, not long after receiving Coventry's maroon and cream livery. It would later be rebodied by Brush and survived as 264 in its new rebodied guise until 1948. (A. J. Owen)

5 (CP 8011)

The second of the former Halifax Corporation double-deckers was number 5 in the Coventry fleet. Despite being purchased as a stop-gap measure because of the damage to the bus fleet in 1940 and 1941, and the lack of available new buses, both of the former Halifax Corporation buses were rebodied. The two former Halifax Corporation buses were rebodied in January 1943 by Brush with MoS style H30/26R bodies that were the same design as that on the rebodied Daimler COG5/60 240, with the square side window in the front dome. The resulting bodywork was very similar to the fifty AEC Regent 661s that were rebodied by Brush between July 1943 and April 1944 for Birmingham City Transport. 5 (CP 8011) is posed for its official photograph at the Brush works in Loughborough in 1943. The strange numbering of the four AEC Regents was simply to use just one of the former Halifax fleet numbers and in 1946 5 was renumbered 265. (Brush)

7 (CP 9070)

Above: Parked up in the middle of the three buses in the back row at Harnall Lane garage yard in 1948, and apparently withdrawn, is former Halifax Joint Committee 107, built in 1931. Acquired in December 1938, this AEC Regent 661 was initially given the fleet number 7 (CP 9070). It kept its Hoyal H26/24RO body when the MoS refused to sanction the rebodying of this bus and CP 9077. 7 was rebuilt during 1943 by Coventry Steel Caravans. The raised section of the 'camel' type roof is clearly visible. 7, later 267, remained in use until 1948. On the right is rebodied AEC Regent 5 (CP 8011), and on the left Daimler CP6 108 (KV 7108). (A. J. Owen)

244 (EVC 244)

Above: In June 1940, three more Daimler COG5/40 single-deckers arrived and were the last of the model to be delivered to a British operator. Numbered 242–244, they had Park Royal B38F bodies and, because of the high seating capacity, very short cabs with the bulkhead moved as far possible as could be accommodated within the 27' 6" length of the bus. The three buses had very short lives in Coventry and were withdrawn along with all the other COG5 single-deckers in 1949. 244 (EVC 244) was sold to Derby Corporation in November 1949 and was given the fleet number 47, although it was only ever part of the service vehicle fleet. It was used as the Transport Committee coach and remained with Derby until it was sold for preservation in March 1973 to Derby Industrial Museum. It was finally lovingly restored to Coventry Transport livery in 2012 under the ownership of Roger Burdett. The former Coventry bus is parked in Ascot Drive garage yard. (A. D. Broughall)

243 (EVC 243)

Opposite below: Whereas most of Coventry's pre-war double-decker fleet were sold for scrap after their service life had ended, the opposite tended to be true with single-deck buses. This was due to them having less use in municipal ownership and therefore lower mileages and less careworn bodywork. 243 (EVC 243), a Daimler COG5/40 with a Park Royal B38F body, was the middle bus of a trio that entered service in June 1940; these were the last pre-war Daimler buses to enter service with any operator. 243, despite its comparative youth, was summarily taken out of service along with all the other fourteen COG5 single-deckers when they were all replaced by sixteen Brush-bodied Daimler CVD6s in 1949. 243 was sold in February 1950 via Irvine, the Salsburgh-based dealer, to Deeside, Ballater, where it joined the 1938-built 206 (DHP 206). It was numbered 7 in the Deeside bus fleet, where it remained in service until about 1962. (D. R. Harvey Collection)

246 (EVC 246)

Above: One of the roads demolished for Trinity Street's construction in 1937 was Great Butcher Row, and a large steel-framed building was built in 1938 to blend in with the genuine medieval Lychgate Cottages to which it was attached. This had a timber-frame jettied frontage, bay windows, balconies, gables and tall brick chimneys. Originally called Priory Gate, for many years this was the premises of Timothy Whites, the chemist. Parked at the junction with Broadgate is 246 (EVC 246). This was the last Daimler COA6 to be built before production stopped after the destruction of Daimler's Radford works on 14 November 1940. 246 was intended for display at the 1939 Commercial Motor Show along with Brush-bodied 245, a Daimler COG5/60, and entered service in January 1940. Neither of these two vehicles are known to be part of a Coventry order and both had chassis numbers not in the range of other Coventry chassis, so one must assume that both were built speculatively and subsequently purchased by Coventry Transport. (R. Marshall)

248 (EVC 248)

Opposite: Turning onto High Street from Broadgate in about 1941 is 248 (EVC 248). It is working on the 2 route to Cheylesmore. The Brush-bodied Daimler COG5/60 in May 1940 is passing the 1930s classically styled National Provincial Bank on the corner of Hertford Street, where Metro-Cammell-bodied Daimler COA6 236 (EHP 236) waits to be noticed by the policeman on point duty. Behind the Rover 14 Sports Saloon, turning into Broadgate, is the gaunt frontage of the destroyed Montague Burton store, while beyond the Standard Flying Twelve motor car standing on the abandoned tram tracks are the almost totally destroyed remains of Smithford Street. (D. R. Harvey Collection)

249 (EVC 249)

Above: The terminus of the 6 bus route was at the Red Lion public house in Ansty Road, Walsgrave-on-Stowe. Parked alongside the pub is 249 (EVC 249), a Daimler CO5/60 with a Brush H29/31R body delivered in November 1940, just before the bombing of 14 November 1940, making it, along with 256, the last of the pre-war buses to be delivered. It only lasted until 1951, becoming the first of the 1940 double-deckers to be withdrawn. (A. A. Cooper)

253 (EVC 253)

Opposite above: Waiting on the forecourt of the Red Lion public house in Ansty Road, Walsgrave-on-Stowe, is one of the last batch of pre-war double-deckers to be delivered. 253 (EVC 253), a Daimler COG5/60, had a Brush H29/31R body and was delivered in November 1940, just as the city was subjected to the terrible air raid on 14/15 November 1940. The bus is at the terminus of the 6 bus route but by this time the bus had been fitted with one of the early Daimler CD6 8.6-litre engines and thus 253 became a COD6. Withdrawn in 1952, it was converted to an open-top tree cutter numbered TC01. (R. Marshall)

254 (EVC 254)

Opposite below: 254 (EVC 254) was barely two months old when it was caught in the 14 November 1940 air raid. It was standing in Pool Meadow bus station when it was blown over by a bomb blast. Lying on its offside, its nearside is virtually blown away. The Brush body on the Daimler COG5/60 chassis was not destroyed and was rebuilt by Brush using many of the surviving body parts. 254 was returned to service in June 1942 and survived until 1952, whereupon it was sold to Birds of Stratford for scrap. (D. R. Harvey Collection)

255 (EVC 255)

Above: Just arrived at the Hales Street entrance to Pool Meadow bus station is Brush-bodied Daimler COG5/60 255 (EVC 255). It entered service in August 1940 and, as with all the 1940 orders, was finished to full pre-war standards. A noticeable feature of all these later Brush bodies built for Coventry were the thicker upper-saloon side body pillars in the front and rear domes. It is parked alongside a Royal Navy recruitment poster featuring the 13,400-ton HMS *Glory* Colossus-class aircraft carrier. (D. F. Parker)

257 (EVC 257)

Above: Another bus to have a waist rail fleet number was 257 (EVC 257). This Daimler COG5/60 had a Brush H29/31R body and was delivered in July 1940, though it did not enter service until October of the same year.

The metal strips around the front destination boxes indicated that the bus was a sixty-seater. The bus is working to Walsgrave (in the east of the city) by way of the Coventry Show, which is being advertised on the slip board in the front lower-saloon window. Behind 257 is 1952-vintage 129 (KVC 129), a Daimler CVD6 with a BCT-style 'New Look' concealed radiator MCCW H31/27R body also working 'To and From the Show'. (D. F. Parker)

256 (EVC 256)

Opposite below: On Tuesday 23 May 1950, 256 (EVC 256) stands in Broadgate at the covered bus shelters with the medieval Trinity church towering over the temporary shops. The bus is working on the 16 route to Green Lane. The Brush-bodied bus was a Daimler COG5/60, but, after the trialling of 240 with the new Daimler CD6 engine in the spring of 1945, a CD6 8.6-litre engine was fitted to 256 and 253 in April 1945, thus becoming a Daimler COD6 chassis. It remained in service in this form until 1956. (A. A. Cooper)

258 (EVC 258)

Above: After its sale to Superb Coaches of Birmingham in July 1953, the former Coventry Transport 258 (EVC 258), a Daimler COG5/60, only lasted fifteen months, despite being in apparently good condition. The bus had its original Brush body destroyed when the bus was bombed in the city centre on 14 November 1940. As a result, 258 was rebodied by Brush in July 1942 with their last pre-war design for Coventry, featuring curved bottom edges to its end windows. This was first tried out on 252 and used on the three AEC Regent o661s of 1942 and the other four 1942 rebodied assorted pre-war Daimlers. (A. M. Wright)

260 (EVC 260)

Opposite below: With the bus crew posing in front of their vehicle, 260 (EVC 260) is parked in Pool Meadow bus station when working on the route to Wyken. This AEC Regent o661 entered service in February 1942 with a Coventry-style Brush H31/29R body built to the Transport Department's pre-war specification. The only anomaly to the congruity of the body design was the rather large, bulbous cab apron, which looked as though it had been built as an afterthought. Seven further AEC Regent o661 chassis were fitted with identical bodies and it was always presumed that they were to become Coventry's 262–268, but at a very late stage they were diverted, with one going to Kingston-upon-Hull Corporation as their 196 (GKH 377), and six somewhat strangely to Midland Red. These were numbered by BMMO as 2441–2446 (GHA 795–800); Midland Red immediately rejected the Coventry seats before delivery, thus allowing them to be fitted to Coventry's Guy Arab Is numbered 285–289 and the solitary rebodied Daimler COA6, 240 (EWK 240). (R. Marshall)

259 (EVC 259)

Above: 259 (EVC 259), one of just ninety-two AEC Regents released by the Ministry of War Transport during 1941 and 1942 under their 'unfrozen' bus chassis release scheme, is standing on Earl Street outside the Council House when working on the 11 route to Binley not long after it was delivered in 1942. 259 was the first of the three unfrozen Coventry-style Brush-bodied 60-seat AEC Regent 0661s allocated to Coventry, arriving in February 1942. These three buses had 7.57-litre direct-injection engines coupled to D124 manual crash gearboxes. Behind the bus is Anslow's furniture shop on the corner of Hay Lane. (W. J. Haynes)

261 (EVC 261)

Seven similar buses, originally intended for Coventry as 262–268, were diverted away from the city fleet with Midland Red getting six and Kingston-upon-Hull Corporation receiving one. The seven AEC Regent 0661s were replaced by one unfrozen Bristol K5G, one unfrozen Leyland Titan TD7 and five Guy Arab Is. 261 (EVC 261) was the last of the trio of unfrozen AEC Regent 0661s and had Brush H31/29R bodies with curved end saloon windows. Originally the destination box on 261 was surrounded with decorative chrome strips to show traffic inspectors that the bus was a sixty-seater. (A. J. Owen)

11 (WJ 520)

WJ 520 was one of the three 1931-vintage Leyland Tiger TS3s originally in the Sheffield
Joint fleet as their 120. Originally it had a Leyland B30R body, but after sale in 1937 to the
City Coach Co. of Brentwood, it was immediately rebodied with a new Duple C32F body.
Coventry obtained 11 (WJ 520) early in 1942, but whereas the other two unrebodied TS3s were
withdrawn in 1945, 11 managed to be renumbered as 263 in February 1946 and was sold to
V & M Coaches of Atherstone in 1948, who ran it for a few months. (R. Marshall)

Hired Wartime Buses

31 (EX 2878)

Among the first buses to enter service after the bombing raid on 14 November 1940 were five Great Yarmouth Corporation United-bodied petrol-engined AEC Regent 661s. The last of these was 31 (EX 2878), which was fitted with an AEC A145 7.4-litre engine. The bodywork had a straight staircase and, although rather square with a hint of a piano front, these were attractive-looking vehicles. These buses went to Coventry in July 1940 at a time when seaside towns were sending surplus buses to industrial areas where the need for them was more pressing. These buses were hired in order to make good on the shortfall in the delivery of new buses, but events resulted in them staying a lot longer than originally envisaged, with thirty-one remaining in Coventry until August 1944. Here, 31 (EX 2878) is working along the coast in its home town on the route to Britannia Pier. (A. D. Packer)

33 (EX3472)

Seven newer oil-engined AEC Regent 0661s with English Electric H26/22R, dating from 1934, also arrived in July 1940 and saw little use until they were pressed into service after the Blitz raid of November 1940. Four were returned to Great Yarmouth in May 1941 after an air raid there, but 33 (EX 3472) remained in Coventry until July 1944. 33 is parked in Regent Road, outside the Regal cinema, Yarmouth, which had opened on New Years Day 1934.

It is showing the 1936 drama film *Suzy* starring Jean Harlow (the original blonde bombshell), Franchot Tone and Cary Grant. The film was partially written by Dorothy Parker and was one of Jean Harlow's last films as she died on 7 July 1937, aged 26. (OS)

81 (WH 4910)

Above: A total of thirty-one buses were on extended loan from Bolton Corporation from March 1941 until February 1942, although there were never more than twenty-five in Coventry at any one time. Bolton's 81 (WH 4910) was a Leyland Titan TD3 with an English ElectricH28/24R body, new in 1933. It arrived immediately after the air raids in Easter Holy Week on the nights of 8 and 10 April 1941, having previously been on loan to Midland Red. It was returned to Bolton in January 1944. (J. Higham)

15 (WH 6857)

Above: Charles Roberts of Horbury, Wakefield were basically railway stock builders who periodically built bus bodies when demand was high and railway wagon construction was at a low ebb. In the mid-1930s, Roberts built a large number of bus bodies and in 1935, they received an order from Bolton Corporation for ten double-deck bodies. 15 (WH 6857) was a Leyland Titan TD4c with a torque convertor gearbox and a fifty-two seat, slightly conservatively styled, six-bay construction body. It stands in Robert's Horbury yard shortly after completion. It also arrived on loan via Midland Red in April 1941 and stayed in Coventry until July 1944. Whatever was said about the gearboxes on these buses was mercifully not recorded. It was the first of the batch but was rebodied by NCB in 1945, though it was withdrawn in 1948. (Charles Roberts)

208 (JN 9528)

Opposite above: A similar loan was made in July 1940 with the borrowing of four further AEC Regent 0661s from Southend Corporation. These were lowbridge English Electric-bodied fifty-three seaters built in 1937. The buses, originally numbered 157–160 in the Southend fleet, were renumbered when just a year old as 207–210, and were renumbered when on loan to Coventry as 20, 8, 9 and 10 by the simple act of painting out part of the Southend fleet number. Thus 208 became Coventry's 8 (JN 9528), and was kept until June 1942. 208 stands in Thorpe Hall Avenue with Thorpe Esplanade and a very old four-masted ship in Thorpe Bay in the distance. The visible tram tracks are part of the service from Southchurch, which was abandoned in July 1938. (OS)

713 (ENC 936)

Three Corporation employees, who were also part of the Home Guard, were on duty at Harnall Lane garage and are standing in front of 713 (ENC 936) in 1938. This was one of three Crossley Mancunians sent by Manchester Corporation on loan to Coventry from April 1941 until August 1944. It had a streamlined Metro-Cammell body framework finished by Manchester Corporation at their Hyde Road works, with distinctive cream livery swoops over the rest of the bright red livery. The Crossley Mancunian had a Crossley VR6, 8,365 cc indirect-injection engine and a constant mesh gearbox. (D. R. Harvey Collection)

49 (RY 7856)

Nearby Leicester City Transport contributed four buses for about two weeks after the Holy Week raids on Tuesday 8 April and Thursday 10 April 1941. Over the two nights, 451 people were killed and over 700 seriously injured. The buses had all been returned before the end of April. All four were antiquated-looking Guy CX six-wheel normal-control chassis with Brush H30/26R bodywork. The last of the quartet was 49 (RY 7856), which was the newest of them, entering service in August 1929. The bus is working on the 24 service in Leicester in about 1937. They really made the indigenous Maudslay ML7s, built in the same year, look modern. (Photomatic)

ST 806 (GO 5137)

Above: ST 806 (GO 5137) was on loan for two years, from December 1942 until December 1944, and was one of only six of these borrowed London Transport STs converted to run on producer gas in Coventry during 1943 and 1944. This bus entered service in May 1931 and survived in service until September 1949, operating from Willesden garage. It is working on a Derby Day special in 1949 to Epsom racecourse, a service which was frequently operated by elderly buses at the end of their working lives. (P. Fidczuk)

970 (CH 6251)

Opposite above: Delivered in 1927, 970 (CH 6251) was one of the six 1927-vintage SOS Qs built for Trent Motor Traction with Brush B37F bodies briefly lent to Coventry Transport in April 1941. Many years earlier, bus 970 waits in Derby's art deco bus station soon after its opening in 1933. It is about to leave on the service to Alfreton. Behind 970 stands the two-year-newer SOS M lower-built 407 (CH 8115). The spoked front wheels reveals that the SOS Q model was not equipped with front brakes. (W. J. Haynes)

ST 481 (GK 5313)

Opposite below: Standing opposite Holy Trinity church in the bombed wasteland that was Broadgate is GK 5312. This was a petrol-engined AEC Regent 661 with an LGOC H28/20R body that had been delivered new to London General as their ST 481 in 1930. It was on loan from July 1942 until August 1944 and is working on a service to Whitley, where the car factories of Humber, Hillman, and Sunbeam-Talbot were located, manufacturing wartime vehicles for the armed services. (A. J. Owen)

Wartime Buses 1942–1945

284 (EKV 284)

The allocation of either unfrozen or wartime Bristol K type chassis to any operator in the Midlands was almost unheard of, with only Coventry Transport and Derby Corporation receiving solitary examples of the Bristol K5G model during 1942, the former being delivered in April and the Derby one in June. 284 (EKV 284) was built with the uncompromising Strachan H30/26R bodywork and was delivered in plain varnished grey, though it did have moquette-covered upholstered seating. It was rebuilt by Nudd Brothers & Lockyer in 1951 and remained in service for another seven years.

Eighty-five unfrozen Bristol K5Gs were built and, while regarded as engineers' buses, they were prone to heavy vibration and 284 was never popular, being frequently used in its latter years as a driver instruction vehicle. It is parked outside the entrance of Harnall Lane garage appearing in need of reconstruction as the lower-saloon waist rail is distinctly uneven. At this stage of its career, 284 was inevitably being employed as a driver training bus. (S. N. J. White)

285 (EKV 285)

In August 1942, the MoS allocated Coventry Transport five Brush-bodied Guy Arab Is. The first of these five was 285 (EKV 285), which had the very early Brush Utility body style, having the unusual H29/27R seating layout and the square front dome side window. The buses came without glazed emergency upper-saloon windows but were painted in full Coventry Transport livery. It still retains the original single line wartime destination box as it works on the route to Willenhall. This bus had its body extensively rebuilt by Nudd Brothers & Lockyer of Kegworth in 1951, involving rubber-mounted saloon windowpanes, new narrow siding vents fitted to four windows on each side of the two saloons and new lower deck pillars. (R. Marshall)

286 (EKV 286)

Travelling along Banner Lane near Tilehill Wood (to the west of the city) in June 1956, with fields as a background, is the unrebuilt 286 (EKV 286). This Guy Arab I, with a Gardner 5LW 7.0-litre engine, had a Brush UH29/27R body and entered service in September 1942. It was eventually rebuilt by Bond as a sixty-seater and was relicensed in June 1953. It still has its original single line wartime destination box which displays RYTON as the destination. It must have been a warm day – not only are the half-drop saloon windows wide open, but the bonnet side panel is wedged open in order to get some air over the hard-worked diesel engine. The staff at Keresley Works were presumably in the midst of some experiments with headlight positions as it retains the original large offside headlight, but the nearside one is a pre-war unit mounted in the low position favoured by Coventry until 1941. (D. F. Parker)

287 (EKV 287)

Parked on Trinity Street and facing into Broadgate is 287 (EKV 287). It is 1 April 1951 and it would only be a matter of a few months before this Brush-bodied Guy Arab I would be sent to Nudd Brothers & Lockyer of Kegworth for a major body rebuild. Brush only bodied a total of seventy-eight Guy Arabs, of which one was a very late Arab II and all the remainder were Arab Is bodied between September 1942 and July 1942. Of these seventy-seven, just twenty-two were highbridge buses and Coventry's 285–289 were the largest single batch, so these buses were a rather rare breed. 287 would survive until 1959, and even then ran for another three years with Walthamstow Education Committee. (A. Cooper)

291 (EKV 291)

Above: Coventry received nine early production Bedford OWB single-deckers, numbered 290–298, in September 1942, being something of a rarity among English municipalities who were normally allocated double-deckers for their usually heavier passenger loadings. 291 (EKV 291) had a Roe B32F and was delivered in a dark-grey livery with wooden slatted seats. These single-deckers provided additional peak-period cover, especially on works services, but otherwise were of limited use. 291 is in Nottingham in 1948 being employed on a private hire duty. (W. J. Haynes)

288 (EKV 288)

Opposite above: 288 (EKV 288) is standing at the rudimentary bus shelters at Tile Hill before going back to the city centre by way of Beech Tree Avenue. The bus is a Guy Arab I, which could be easily distinguished by the short front wings, whereas the Arab II model had curved-ended mudguards. The Brush body was rebuilt by Bond of Wythenshawe in 1953. The rebuilds had double-thickness lower-deck front-corner pillars, sliding vents and two side-by-side destination indicators. About to overtake the bus is a Standard Eight, while travelling in the opposite direction is a Morris Minor convertible, both products of the mid-1950s Midlands car industry. (C. W. Routh)

289 (EKV 289)

Opposite below: Nearside views of any of the 1942 Brush-bodied Guy Arab Is are quite rare. 289 (EKV 289) stands in Harnall Lane garage yard in around 1953, not long before it was sent to S. H. Bond for rebuilding. It is carrying a famous advertisement for 'SAY CWS AND SAVE', which was used between 1952 and 1956. When it was first delivered, 289 came in a light-red and cream livery.

It lasted until 1958 before being sold to AMCC, a dealer in east London who, by 1961, eventually exported 289 to Autoprevoz, Mostar in Yugoslavia as that operator's fleet number 225, and re-registered as MO-10-68. Behind it is 368 (EKV 968), a Duple-bodied Daimler CWA6 of 1944 that had been rebodied in 1951 by Charles Roe. (S. E. Letts)

298 (EKV 298)

The Bedford OWB chassis were fitted with MoWT-designed bodies. 298 (EKV 298) had a Roe B32F body, which could be distinguished from the products of other OWB coachbuilders' products by the thin trim at the top of the front destination box. The body contracts were fulfilled by Duple, Mulliners, Scottish Motor Traction and Charles Roe. Roe built 240 bodies, which was the smallest of all the MoS contracts and fulfilled between July 1942 and July 1943 when the Leeds-based company returned to exclusively building double-deckers. 298 was withdrawn in 1948 and sold via a Coventry-based dealer to Ley of St Buryan, Cornwall, who operated the bus for ten years until August 1958. It is parked in Penzance on 16 August 1950 in the company of an elderly Gilford AS6. (J. Cull)

299 (EKV 299)

299 (EKV 299) arrived in Coventry in November 1942 in a light grey livery with red leather upholstered seating, but with an unglazed upper salon emergency window. This was the solitary unfrozen Leyland Titan TD7 allocated by the MoWT to Coventry. The bus had two drawbacks; firstly, it was a Leyland and there were no Leylands in the fleet save for the ones on loan. Also, it was a TD7 model, which had a very large flywheel and consequently a very slow gearchange which made it unpopular with the traffic department.

It had a Northern Counties lowbridge body with a side gangway, which was also a disadvantage in urban operating conditions. This metal-framed body was an interim style based on the last Northern Counties pre-war design, but with many Utility features such as square front and rear domes and a limited number of opening windows. After a few months in Coventry in an agreed exchange with Middlesbrough Corporation, 299 in 1942 was sold to the Teesside municipality in May 1943. In exchange, Coventry received a lowbridge Brush-bodied Guy Arab II that was numbered 330 (EKV 930) as the chassis conformed to Coventry's standard wartime bus. It is with Paton of Renfrew in Clydebank, who owned it from 1949 until late 1955, as their fleet number 11. (J. C. Walker)

300 (EKV 300)

Above: 300 (EKV 300) was delivered to Coventry in November 1942 in a dark-grey livery and red rexine covered seats and were painted in the full Coventry livery by 1945. It was rebuilt by Coventry Transport in 1947 as only the second wartime rebuild undertaken by the Transport Department at Keresley Works. This was because some Massey bodies, including this one, suffered badly from being built with unseasoned wood and required urgent reconstruction. It was eventually rebuilt by Nudd Brothers in 1951, who only left the curved bottom of the windscreen as a clue to its Massey origins. It is travelling along Banner Lane on the 13 service to Ryton. (R. H. G. Simpson)

302 (EKV 302)

Above: This Guy Arab I was fitted with a Weymann metal-framed streamlined body intended for Manchester Corporation. 302 (EKV 302) was the first of four such bodies delivered to Coventry. Ironically, due to the Blitz of Daimler's Radford works on 14 November 1940, forty-three Daimler COG5 chassis intended for Manchester Corporation were destroyed, although Metro-Cammell had built most of the frames for them. With the unavailability of new chassis and components, the remaining frames were diverted from Manchester by the MoWT, who had them sent to Weymann of Addlestone for completion. They were then all mounted on Guy Arab I chassis and allocated to Coventry Corporation (EKV 302–305), Midland General (HRA 815 and 924), Midland Red (GHA 923, 924), Newport Corporation (DDW 33, 34) and Sheffield Corporation (HWA 578, 582, 679–681).

The conductor appears to be getting a newspaper from the driver of 302 (EKV 302), the first of the four Manchester-styled Weymann-bodied Guys allocated to Coventry Transport. Delivered in February 1943, the smooth front profile of this bus and 305 (EKV 305) was exactly the same as those Daimler COG5s that were delivered to Manchester Corporation. (R. T. Wilson)

303 (EKV 303)

Opposite below: The advertisement on the wall of Pool Meadow bus station is for the Majestic Ballroom. Situated at 51 Primrose Hill Street, the building had first opened as the Globe Picture Theatre in 1914. Closing in 1956, it re-opened in 1957 as the Majestic. It usually had resident big bands such as the Wylie Price Orchestra with their singer Jean Hudson, as listed on the billposter. During the afternoons for the next four years the Majestic had rock 'n' roll dances while the evenings were advertised as modern dance nights. This dates the photograph of bus 303 (EKV 303) to between those dates. The bus is one of the four Guy Arab Is fitted with Manchester Corporation-style bodies completed by Weymann to pre-war standards of equipment and delivered to Coventry Transport in an all-over grey livery in April 1943. Fifteen bodies of this type were mounted on Guy Arab I chassis and Coventry Transport had four of them. Like the Majestic Ballroom, 303 was withdrawn in 1961. (D. R. Harvey Collection)

304 (EKV 304)

Above: Working on the Willenhall route on Saturday 18 August 1951 is Guy Arab I Gardner 5LW-engined 304 (EKV 304). The Weymann H30/26R body is looking very smart in its early post-war maroon and cream livery, with the upper-saloon guttering picked out in cream, as opposed to the original dark-grey livery in which it was delivered in April 1943. Both 303 and 304 differed from the other two Manchester streamlined bodies as they had a broken offside profile with the top deck slightly overhanging the driver's windscreen. This suggests that the body was intended to be for the 1940 contract for Crossley Mancunians chassis, though construction on these was not even started, despite Metro-Cammell having completed the body framework. (A. Cooper)

306 (EKV 306)

Opposite below: Standing in Harnall Lane garage yard in about 1958 is 306 (EKV 306). This Guy Arab I had been rebuilt by Nudd Brothers & Lockyer in 1951, leaving only the driver's offside cab windows and windscreen as a clue that the body had originally been built by Weymann. The bus arrived in Coventry in January 1943 in a dark-grey livery with green rexine seats and would remain in service until 1958, being replaced by Daimler CVG6s registered in the VWK series whose arrival largely saw off all the Guy Arabs in the fleet. This must have been a relief to Coventry's bus drivers as all their Guys had the usual four-speed sliding mesh gearboxes but with the third and fourth gear positions away from the driver where normally first and second gears would have been. (R. H. G. Simpson)

305 (EKV 305)

Above: In its last few weeks in service, 305 (EKV 305), a Guy Arab I, carries a groaningly full load out of Broadgate on the route to Radford on 3 September 1959, the day that your writer started grammar school. Delivered in an all-over dark-grey livery, it was repainted in the full Coventry livery in 1945 with the cream bands on the Weymann bodies reflecting the swooping livery that it was intended to have in Manchester. The bodywork had been well looked after by Keresley Works and was never rebuilt, though it was reseated in 1954 using the seats from the long withdrawn 111 (KV 7111), one of the 1934-vintage Daimler CP6s. (A. J. Douglas)

308 (EKV 308)

Above: The next Weymann bodies were composite-construction to MoWT specification and there were four of them. 308 (EKV 308) was a Guy Arab I with the usual Gardner 5LW 7.0-litre engine and had entered service in January 1943, painted in an unrelieved dark grey livery with rexine covered seating. The bus was never rebodied but was reconditioned by the Transport Department at Keresley Works during September 1951 and again rebuilt by the corporation in December 1955. The bodywork retained the Utility look even after these two rebuilds; the only clue to these reconstructions was the lack of front upper-saloon window hopper ventilators, and that there were six half-drop side windows in each saloon rather than the original two. It was a testament to the in-house rebuilding that it was one of the last eleven Guy Arabs to remain in use, surviving until 1961. 308 is standing at the Tile Hill route bus shelters in Pool Meadow bus station. (D. R. Harvey Collection)

309 (EKV 709)

Opposite below: Grey wartime buses as far as the eye can see! 309 (EKV 309) on the right was, like the next four buses, a Guy Arab I, a model that could usually be distinguished from the later and more numerous Arab II by the plain front wings without the curved front edge. 309 had a Weymann body distinguishable by its flat-faced between-decks paneling and had an unglazed rear emergency window. The second bus is 311 (EKV 711), a Park Royal example with the small angled panel section below the windscreen. The next bus is 310 (EKV 710), another Park Royal-bodied vehicle, and the final identifiable bus in the line-up is 301 (EKV 301), fitted with a Massey body. The remaining buses are painted in various variations of the standard maroon and cream Coventry Transport livery. (D. R. Harvey Collection)

310 (EKV 710)

Above: After its Park Royal UH30/26R body had been rebuilt in the summer of 1950 by Nudd Brothers & Lockyer, 310 (EKV 310) came back from Kegworth transformed. The rebuilt body had new lower-deck pillars, while the windows on both decks were set in rubber mouldings and new sliding vents were fitted to four windows on each side of both saloons. Additionally, the front upper-saloon windows were fixed, with the original wartime opening ventilators being discarded. The only clue to the origins of the body was the small angled ledge below the windscreen that was a feature of the wartime Park Royal body. 310 (EKV 710) is in Pool Meadow bus station when working on the 10 route to Browns Green. (D. R. Harvey Collection)

313 (EKV 713)

Above: About to be overtaken by an early post-war Ford Anglia EO4A saloon on 29 September 1951 is 313 (EKV 713), a Park Royal-bodied Guy Arab I working on the 13 route. It is in Banner Lane, just after the Broad Lane junction near Tilehill Wood. The bus had been rebuilt with twin front destination boxes, a glazed rear emergency window in the upper saloon and two extra half drop windows in each saloon, but during the following year it would go to Bond of Wythenshawe, near Manchester, to be completely rebuilt. 313 returned to service in February 1953 and this extensive reconstruction would give the bus an extra five years of use. (A. Cooper)

316 (EKV 816)

Above: Bus number 316 (EKV 816) is parked at the top of Trinity Street at the entrance to Broadgate. Behind the bus are the half-timbered Lychgate Cottages, dating to the fifteenth century, while to the left of the bus are the premises of Timothy Whites, the chemist, housed in a timber-framed, bay-windowed, mock-Jacobean building dating from 1938, originally called Priory Gate. 316 was the first of a batch of five vehicles numbered 316–320. The bus is a Daimler CWG5s, with a Gardner 5LW engine and a Duple UH30/26R body, which was delivered in March 1943. Exactly 100 of the CWG5 model were built at the Courtaulds factory in Whitmore Reans, Wolverhampton, which had been requisitioned from by the Ministry of Supply and then occupied by Daimlers. Sixty of the CWG5s were bodied as highbridge buses. The number was split equally between Duple and Massey, and Coventry had examples of both. 316 is in original condition except that it had been repainted in 1945 from the light-grey delivery livery. It was rebuilt by Nudd brothers & Lockyer in 1951 and renumbered as late as November 1963 as 416. (S. N. J. White)

314 (EKV 314)

Opposite below: The penultimate Guy Arab I to be delivered to Coventry Transport was 314 (EKV 314), which was delivered in January 1943. It had a Park Royal UH30/26R body and, when new, had a dark-grey livery, green rexine seats and an unglazed upper-saloon emergency window. The bus had been fitted with an extra pair of half-drop windows in each saloon, but was otherwise in original condition. Five of the six of the Park Royal-bodied buses were, perhaps surprisingly, the first wartime Coventry buses to be sent to Nudd Brothers & Lockyer for rebuilding. This occurred in 1950 and was returned in 1951. The bus survived after this extensive refurbishment for another ten years. (S. N. J. White)

317 (EKV 817)

Left: The Daimler CWG5 was perhaps the least austere of all the wartime bus chassis models and was similar to the COG5 model. Although the chromium-plated radiator was now painted, and it was equipped with small military-style headlamps, it did retain the Daimler fluid flywheel, and the pre-selector gearbox and flexible engine mountings reduced the vibrations produced by the five-cylinder Gardner 5LW engine. 317 (EKV 817), delivered in April 1943, had originally been intended to have been part of a batch of Park Royal-bodied Guy Arab Is numbered 316–321, but those were transferred elsewhere and Coventry got its CWG5s.

317 was reconstructed by Bond of Wythenshawe, but underneath the rubber-mounted windows and sliding saloon ventilators was a Duple UH30/26R body. This rebuilding had been completed in 1953 and the bus is posed immediately after this work had been completed. The Bond rebuilds could be distinguished from the Nudd examples by the square-shaped front dome side windows that followed the corner body pillar. (Bond)

318 (EKV 818)

Above: Most of the Coventry Transport wartime buses that were sold to the dealer Passenger Vehicle Sales of Upminster towards the end of 1958 were resold to independent operators or contractors for further use. In this capacity rarely more than two or three years' further service was squeezed out of the bus and despite its tidy appearance, 318 (EKV 818) was no exception. Knightswood Coaches of Watford used 318 from November 1958 until 1960 and it is seen being used on hire to Ronsway Coaches, leaving Wembley Stadium fully laden with football supporters. This Daimler CWG5 is in company with WXC 338, a 1959-built Harrington C37F-bodied Bedford SB8 owned by Fallowfield & Britten. (R. H. G. Simpson)

320 (EKV 820)

Right: Parked in Pool Meadow bus station in around 1948 is 320 (EKV 820). The Duple body of this Daimler CWG5 is in largely original condition with only the opening saloon windows being altered from the standard half drop style to a somewhat homemade sliding arrangement. This was the first wartime bus to be delivered with a glazed rear emergency window. Of the seven CWG5s delivered to Coventry Transport, three of the Duple-bodied examples were withdrawn in the late spring of 1958, but whereas the other two had quite short lives with other operators, 320 was sold in July 1958 to Wessex Coaches of Bristol. (D. R. Harvey Collection)

320 (EKV 820)

Above: After it was withdrawn in 1958, Coventry Transport's 320 (EKV 820), a Daimler CWG5 with a Bond-rebuilt Duple UH30/26R body, was sold to Wessex Coaches of Bristol. It was repainted in their drab all-over blue livery and used as part of their contract bus fleet, ferrying workmen to the nuclear power station construction site at Hinckley Point, five miles north of Bridgwater in north Somerset. During this time it would have carried the Taylor Woodrow fleet name, as they were the contractor at the construction site. The former Coventry 320 was withdrawn in May 1963 and then used, in cut-down form, as a tree lopper and towing vehicle until finally being withdrawn in November 1964. It is parked, out of use, with the body cut off behind the rear axle and on the top deck only the front dome and first bay are extant. Alongside it is a Weymann-bodied AEC Regent III. (R. F. Mack)

321 (EKV 821)

Above: 321 (EKV 821) was the first of two Massey-bodied Daimler CWG5s and was delivered in an all-over red livery during July 1943, some five months after the other twin 322. The Massey bodywork was uncompromisingly gaunt and angular, thus making it very recognisable. They built seventeen bodies on the Guy Arab I but, unfortunately, the wartime products of this Pemberton-based bodybuilder were extremely variable and dependent on the quality of the ash wood with which they were supplied. In April 1949, Daimler CWG5 321 appeared completely reconstructed with the pillars and bulkhead renewed or replaced. Four sliding narrow vents replaced the two half-drop windows on each saloon, but the wartime narrow hopper type vents on the front upper-saloon windows were retained. Two side-by-side destination boxes replaced the original single aperture, but most importantly the bus was reseated to an H31/29R layout. Despite all of these modifications, the angular Massey body features remained recognisable. 342, a Weymann-bodied Daimler CWA6, was also rebuilt as a sixty-seater. 321 was renumbered 421 in November 1963 and was withdrawn the following month before being first sold to Smith of Long Itchington and then Priory Coaches of Leamington, who operated the bus until February 1968. It is manoeuvring its way around the car park alongside Pool Meadow bus station. (Vectis)

322 (EKV 822)

Opposite above: Parked at the end of the central row of bus shelters in Pool Meadow bus station is 322 (EKV 822). This was the last of the Daimler CWG5s allocated to Coventry in March 1943 and had a MoS-style Massey H30/26R body. It was one of just six wartime buses to survive long enough to have 100 added to the fleet number in order not to clash with the 313–337 batch of MCCW-bodied Daimler CVG6s that entered service in November and December 1963. Renumbered as 422, this bus only operated for four months before it was taken out of service and sold to Milleons, a Barnsley scrap dealer. (H. W. Peers)

325 (EKV 825)

Below: Weymann-bodied Guy Arab II 325 (EKV 825) is at Addlestone when the bus was new in June 1943. It is painted in an all-over varnished grey livery and had wooden slatted seating, but it did have the luxury of having a glazed rear emergency window in the upper saloon. 325 was repainted in maroon and cream in 1945, and after another six years was sent to Nudd Brothers & Lockyer for rebuilding in January 1951 before being returned to service on 1 June 1951. This rebuilding enabled Coventry to get another ten years' service out of 325 at a time when many other operators had already given up with their wartime buses and sold them on to scrap merchants. (D. R. Harvey Collection)

327 (EKV 827)

Above: Making its way into Pool Meadow bus station is the Nudd Brother & Lockyer rebuilt 327 (EKV 827). These extensive reconstructions somehow looked taller and thinner than the original bodywork, which in this case was built by Weymann. After the last pre-war Daimler COA6s had been withdrawn in 1956, the wartime Guys were reduced to mainly peak-hour extras, which is why 327 is showing 'SERVICE EXTRA' on the right-hand destination box. The buses were always a bit sluggish with their Gardner 5LW 7.0-litre engines, and the crash gearboxes were something of a hindrance to an inexperienced driver, but they did have a splendidly noisy exhaust sound. 327 lasted until 1961, which was the last year that the wartime Guys were in service. (R. F. Mack)

328 (EKV 828)

Opposite above: Climbing up Trinity Street on 3 September 1959 is 328 (EKV 828). This was a Guy Arab II with a Weymann UH30/26R that entered service in July 1943. The rebuilding work on this bus was again undertaken by Nudd Brother & Lockyer at Kegworth, but it was somewhat strange that the driver's door and offside cab glazing was left in largely original condition, thus helping to identify the original bodybuilder. The Bond rebuilds had the cab glazing rebuilt to match the rest of the rubber-mounted glazing. The bus is about to overtake a late 1956 Portsmouth-registered Austin A35 four-door saloon while being followed by a 1934 Standard. (A. J. Douglas)

329 (EKV 829)

Opposite below: There was a rugged charm about Weymann wartime composite MoS-type bodies, as exemplified by 329 (EKV 829). The Weymann body design could be identified by the cab door and the associated glazing extending up to the upper-saloon floor level. This Guy Arab II stands in Pool Meadow bus station with the old Swanswell City Gate, dating from around 1440, guarding the entrance and the poster advertising all-in wrestling on the wall behind the bus shelters. 329 entered service in September 1942 but was repainted in Coventry's normal livery in 1945. It was reseated with seats from pre-war buses in 1950 and in was sent to S. H. Bond for rebuilding in 1952. (D. R. Harvey Collection)

330 (EKV 930)

Above: 330 (EKV 930), a Guy Arab I, was the only wartime Guy to be fitted with the large 8.4-litre Gardner 6LW engine. This was because the vehicle was intended for Middlesbrough Corporation and their terrain required the larger engine option rather than the more normal 7.0-litre Gardner 5LW engine. It had a Brush L27/28R body and was exchanged with Coventry 299 (EKV 299), a Leyland Titan TD7 with a NCME L27/26R body, in May 1943 and was delivered directly to Coventry. Surprisingly, despite having a lowbridge body, it remained in service until 1953. It is on St James's Lane, Willenhall during October 1952. (A. A. Cooper)

332 (EKV 932)

Above: Speeding along Banner Lane on 13 September 1951 when working on the 13 route is Park Royal-bodied Guy Arab II 332 (EKV 932). The bus had received the pair of standard destination blinds in July 1949 when it was reseated to a H31/29R seating layout. It was later rebuilt by Bond in 1953 and the seating capacity was retained. The bus had entered service in October 1943, by which time the Park Royal body design had been altered to the Relaxed style, though external differences between this and the original design were difficult to easily identify. (A. Cooper)

330 (EKV 930)

Opposite below: Yes, this really was Coventry Transport's 330 (EKV 930)! This had been a stock Guy chassis that had been intended for Middlesbrough Corporation but was swapped with Coventry's 299 (EKV 299) before it was delivered, coming directly to Coventry. It had been intended to be rebuilt by Bond, but when it was realised that it had a non-standard lowbridge layout it was replaced on the contract list by Brush-bodied Daimler CWA6 361. After withdrawal in 1953, the chassis was sold to Dodd's of Troon, who rebodied it with a new, somewhat flamboyantly styled, Associated Coach Builders' FC37F body. It remained with Dodd's until 1966. (R. F. Mack)

333 (EKV 933)

Above: The Nudd Brothers & Lockyer rebuilding of the Park Royal body on Guy Arab II 333 (EKV 333) in 1951 had only recently taken place as the bus stands in Banner Lane near Tilehill Wood. The paintwork on 333 is positively gleaming and between the decks shows a reflection of a tree on the opposite side of the road which at first sight makes one of the panels look damaged. It is working on the 13 route works service to the Armstrong Whitworth Aircraft factory at Bagington. The remnants of the original Park Royal bodywork can be identified on the offside of the driver's cab. (R. Marshall)

334 (EKV 934)

Opposite above: Manoeuvring its way around the car park alongside the distant Pool Meadow bus station is Nudd Brothers & Lockyer rebuild 334 (EKV 934). This Guy Arab II had the usual Gardner 5LW 7.0-litre engine and, around the cab area, vestiges of its original Park Royal body can still be identified. It had been rebuilt in 1951 with rubber-mounted windows, sliding ventilators and plain glass upper-saloon front windows. The bus has arrived in Pool Meadow bus station after working on the 8 route from Walsgrave. 334 (EKV 934) had been delivered with wooden slatted seats and was repainted in full Coventry Corporation livery by 1945. (Vectis)

336 (EKV 936)

Opposite below: In February 1944, Coventry Transport received its first Daimler CWA6 chassis, arriving as 336 (EKV 336). It, and the next two buses in the fleet, were bodied by Duple with a seating arrangement of UH30/26R. In a pre-delivery photograph, 336 is painted in a red oxide and cream livery that followed the standard Coventry layout, but, though they have a glazed rear upper-saloon emergency window, they had wooden slatted seats. These were the first of some forty-six CWA6 to be allocated to Coventry Transport and were very close to their own unique pre-war Daimler COA6 chassis type. 336 was rebodied with a new Roe H31/25R body in 1951. (Duple)

338 (EKV 938)

Above: The second new wartime Daimler model was designated the CWA6. The chassis had the AEC A173 six-cylinder engine with a swept volume of 7.58 litres. This had been used in the 1930s Daimler COA6 buses that had been Coventry Corporation's standard, and the CWA6 was derived from them, but the engine installation lacked the rubber mountings used in the CWG5, with the engine being bolted directly to the frame. This was only noticeable at high engine revs in each gear as it could produce teeth-rattling vibrations. 338 (EKV 938) was sent to Nudd Brothers & Lockyer for rebuilding in September 1951, with double-thickness corner pillars for extra rigidity. In its rebuilt form, 338 is parked at the top of Trinity Street when working on the 20 route to the railway station, with the vestiges of its Duple body remaining in the area of the driver's cab door. (D. R. Harvey Collection)

339 (EKV 939)

Opposite above: 339 (EKV 939) is parked just beyond the 1920s-built Council House on Earl Street in the lay-by, in front of the proposed Herbert Art Gallery and Museum site, on 21 July 1951 while working on the Stoke Heath route. In December 1949, CCT started to rebuild all the Northern Counties-bodied CWA6s at Keresley Works which, due to having metal-framed bodywork, theoretically required less drastic rebuilding work. When new, they were fitted with extremely uncomfortable wartime slatted seats, which were all later replaced during reconstruction with retrimmed green and red rexine covered seats from withdrawn Brush-bodied Daimler COA6s. 339 was the first of the NCME-bodied buses to be reconditioned, possibly because it was one of the two that had a wooden top-deck framework mounted on top of the normal metal-framed lower deck. (A. Cooper)

340 (EKV 940)

Opposite below: In February and March 1944, Coventry Transport received three Northern Counties metal-framed bodies on Daimler CWA6s. These buses were apparently originally allocated to another Midland municipality who did not want the metal-framed bodies and they were reallocated to Coventry. The middle one of the three was 340 (EKV 940). It is standing in Pool Meadow bus station when working on the 6 service to Walsgrave while wearing a mid-1950s advertisement for the Co-operative Society. The bus was withdrawn in 1958 and sold for spares to Wessex of Bristol. (D. R. Harvey Collection)

341 (EKV 941)

Standing at the Lenton's Lane and Alderman's Green bus shelter in Pool Meadow bus station is Northern Counties-bodied Daimler CWA6 341 (EKV 941). Northern Counties had received permission to continue using metal-framed construction for its wartime bus bodies and included pressed window panes with rounded corners and a slight overhang of the top deck above the windscreen. The result was a distinctively styled bus which, in its earlier form, had a severe appearance to the upper deck and roof with very square front and rear domes. These would be gradually softened and made more round so that, by about 1948, the early post-war Northern Counties bodies were still recognisably based on the original wartime design. (R. A. Mills)

342 (EKV 942)

The arrival of new buses throughout 1944 enabled Coventry Transport to return most of the buses hired in after the devastating raids of three years earlier. All those going back to municipals operators were duly given mechanical overhauls. New in March 1943, 342 (EKV 942), a Daimler CWA6 with a Weymann UH30/26R body, delivered in grey livery and wooden slatted seating, had been the first wartime Coventry bus to be rebuilt in December 1947 when, as well as receiving the standard twin front destination blinds, it also was reseated to a sixty-seater with a rear-facing five seats attached to the bulkhead. It is parked in Pool Meadow bus station in about 1960.

When, in 1952, further contracts were issued for rebuilding more wartime buses, the contract was issued to East Lancashire Coachbuilders of Bridlington. Circumstances dictated that of the five buses intended to go to East Lancs, only 342 and 309 were actually completed in Bridlington, with the former having what was virtually a new upper saloon. (Vectis)

346 (EKV 946)

Above: 346 (EKV 946) was numbered out of sequence, being delivered in November 1943 as the sixth member of the 331–335 batch of Park Royal-bodied Guy Arab II. The surrounding numbers occupied by variously bodied Daimler CWA6s were delivered between March and May 1944, thus leaving 346 in splendid fleet number isolation for about seven months. It had been delivered in full Coventry livery and with wooden slatted seats.

346 waits in Pool Meadow bus station before leaving for Canley on the 18A route, about twelve months before being rebuilt by Bond of Wythenshawe in 1951. (R. Marshall)

344 (EKV 944)

Opposite above: The use of slip boards was becoming something of a rarity in the 1960s, but 344 (EKV 944) is carrying one for Tile Hill South in the lower-saloon front window as it lies in repose at Harnall Lane. This was the last of Coventry Transport's wartime buses to remain in service and was not taken out of service until August 1964. 344 was another Daimler CWA6 with a Weymann body and had arrived in Coventry in February 1944. It had been rebuilt by S. H. Bond of Wythenshawe, some 8 miles south of Manchester. (C. D. Mann)

345 (EKV 945)

Opposite below: The combination of Weymann bodies mounted on Daimler CWA6 chassis was only found on Coventry's 342–345. The last of this quartet was 345 (EKV 945), which is seen parked in Pool Meadow bus station after working on the 3 route soon after it had been rebuilt, with a full set of Coventry-type seating, two extra half-drop windows in each saloon and destination boxes, in March 1951. It had been delivered in a red oxide and cream livery, yet within a year it had been sent to Bond of Wythenshawe for a total rebuild. (S. E. Letts)

347 (EKV 947)

Above: Travelling along Warwick Road at The Quadrant is 347 (EKV 947). It is on its way to the nearby Coventry railway station on 15 May 1950. It has still got its single aperture destination box. Behind the bus on the left is Hertford Street, which the bus had travelled along on its way from the distant Broadgate. The bus is a Northern Counties-bodied Daimler CWA6 dating from May 1944 and was delivered in a grey livery with wooden slatted seating. They were stored unlicensed in Harnall Lane for some time with only chalked-on fleet numbers, but were repainted in a simplified Coventry maroon and cream livery before entering service. Because of its metal-framed bodywork, 347 was only rebuilt once by CCT in 1952. (R. T. Wilson)

348 (EKV 948)

Opposite above: Standing in Pool Meadow bus station in about 1960 is 348 (EKV 948), which has arrived from Canley on the 11 route. The bus is a Daimler CWA6, with a Northern Counties UH30/26R body which had been rebuilt at Keresley Works with a full set of sliding saloon ventilators, the elimination of the ventilators in the upper-saloon front windows and the replacement of the wooden slatted seats with cushioned metal-framed seating from withdrawn pre-war buses, in this case using new Lister moquette. (Vectis)

349 (EKV 949)

Opposite below: Arriving in Pool Meadow bus station on the 10 route is 349 (EKV 949), a Corporation rebuilt Daimler CWA6 with a Northern Counties body. It is being followed by 192 (SKV 192), a Daimler CVG6 with a MCCW H33/27R body dating from 1956. 349 was another of the thirteen Coventry Transport Northern Counties-bodied buses that were all rebuilt by the Corporation rather than being sent to be refurbished by an outside bodybuilder. This was due in the main to the bodies being metal-framed and therefore not subject to the sometimes awful wood rot that had become common on some of the bodies supplied, especially those built by Massey. 349 was the last of Coventry's Northern Counties CWA6s to be rebuilt at Keresley Works in early 1953. (Vectis)

351 (EKV 951)

Above: On Saturday 18 August 1951, a few months after being fitted with upholstered seats and twin front destination boxes, 351 (EKV 951) basks in the summer sunshine at the top of Trinity Street. It is working on the 21 route from Wood End in the east of the city and will shortly move on to Coventry railway station off Warwick Road. Repaints at this time were still receiving cream-painted guttering above the upper-saloon front windows. This Northern Counties-bodied Daimler CWA6 has yet to have its final rebuilding as it still has only a pair of half-drop windows in each saloon. (A. Cooper)

353 (EKV 953)

Above: The crew of 353 (EKV 953) pose alongside the nearside mudguard of their NCME-bodied Daimler CWA6 in Broadgate. Behind them is Broadgate House, known originally to planners as 'Block B'. It was constructed from 1948 on the land between the location of the marketplace and Smithford Street, both of which had largely been obliterated by the German air raid on the night of 14 November 1940. Built as a mixed development of offices, shops and restaurants, it was one of very few Festival of Britain-style commercial buildings built at the time. It was erected as part of Sir Donald Gibson's 'influential and pioneering' post-war redevelopment of the city centre 'embodying the progressive architectural ideology of the era' and was officially opened in May 1953, having cost almost £400,000 to build. It was given Grade II listed status in 2013. The replacement Owen Owen department store officially opened on 1 October the following year on the other side of the square, which was developed as Broadgate. (R. Marshall)

352 (EKV 952)

Opposite below: It is strange that there is such a dearth of nearside front photographs of Coventry Transports buses, but this photograph of 352 (EKV 952) clearly reveals the slightly overhanging upper deck and the matching 45-degree angled edges of the canopy and the rear entrance. The bodywork design was as severe as the products of Massey Brothers, though their method of construction ensured a long life without much structural reconstruction. By now fitted with sliding saloon ventilators, upholstered seating and a pair of destination blinds, 352 is near Pool Meadow bus station when working on the 8 route and is being followed by a 1953 Vauxhall Velox. (C. W. Routh)

354 (EKV 954)

Above: 354 (EKV 954), a Daimler CWA6 with a Northern Counties UH30/26R body, is parked near to Pool Meadow bus station after working on the 8 route. The body of this bus was rebuilt by the Corporation in 1952, with the obvious replacement of the original half-drop saloon windows with sliding ventilators. The CWA6 model was the wartime version of the Daimler COA6 model that had only been specified by Coventry Transport. Both models had the AEC A173 7.58-litre engine and both could be distinguished by the single front positioned access hole on the bonnet side plate. This gave admission to the oil-filler cap, enabling garage fitters and mechanics to top up the oil without having to lift the complete bonnet assembly.

Behind 354 is 14 (FHP 140), one of the first post-war Daimler CVA6s that received the same type of AEC oil engine. (Vectis)

355 (EKV 955)

Opposite above: Stuck in traffic and following a Morris Minor 1000, and in turn being followed by a 1939 Ford Anglia and a 1956 Standard Ten, is 355 (EKV 955), a Daimler CWA6 with a rebuilt Northern Counties body. It is passing Coventry Theatre in Hales Street, which had changed its name from Coventry Hippodrome in 1955. The out-of-service bus is travelling towards Pool Meadow bus station, where it will start its rush hour duty for by this date. The CWA6 were usually only being used as peak time extras. (R. F. Mack)

356 (EKV 956)

Opposite below: As the delivery van driver closes the rear doors of his Bedford CA van, 356 (EKV 956), in its last few months of service, travels along Hales Street as it approaches Pool Meadow bus station on 11 June 1963. 356 was the last of the ten Northern Counties Daimler CWA6s delivered during May and June of 1944 and was duly rebuilt with new cushioned seating in 1949, and then rebuilt in 1952 to have a destination display that conformed to the required Coventry standard. (W. Ryan)

358 (EKV 958)

Above: The last wartime flourish of Guy Arab IIs to be allocated by the Ministry of Supply to Coventry was 358 (EKV 958), the second of a quartet of Strachan UH30/26R bodies to be allocated to Coventry Transport in January 1945. These were the last buses to be given EKV registration letters. These had originally been issued in March 1941 but, due to the low numbers of new vehicles available for civilians to purchase new and subsequently register, it was only replaced in May 1944. 358 is running empty back to Harnall Lane garage and swings out of Broadgate into Trinity Street. Broadgate was a square at this time in name only, having permanent buildings on two sides.

The square, including the garden island, had been established long before this time, having been opened by Princess Elizabeth (later Queen Elizabeth II) on 22 May 1948. This was followed by the unveiling of William Reid Dick's £20,000 bronze Godiva statue on 22 October 1949. By 1955, the Hotel Leofric and the upper end of the precinct had also reached completion and the new Coventry was beginning to take shape. (A. J. Douglas)

359 (EKV 959)

Opposite above: A damp day in Broadgate in 1958 shows 359 (EKV 959), a Strachan-bodied Guy Arab II delivered in January 1945, parked on the right outside the temporary single-storey shops in Broadgate. This is working on the service to Green Lane. Emerging from the scrum of buses in Trinity Street is identical bus 358 (EKV 958). The unique reverse-liveried post-war 'White Lady' of the fleet, 100 (GKV 100), the solitary Crossley, a DD42/7T model with a Metro-Cammell H31/27R body, is pulling across the road when about to run back to Harnall Lane garage. Behind it is the large Owen Owen Store at the top of Trinity Street, which was opened in 1954 having replaced the ill-fated 1938 department store destroyed in the air raid of November 1940. (C. W. Routh)

360 (FDU 60)

Below: Coventry's very last Guy Arab II was delivered in February 1945 and was the first bus to have the new FDU registration letters. Parked in Pool Meadow bus station working on a football special is 360, (FDU 60), a Nudd Brothers & Lockyer rebuild based on a Strachan body. Strachan bodies were not very robust and required an urgent rebuild after only six years of service. One feature retained on all the wartime buses was the nut guard ring on the offside front wheel; this was used to assist drivers to climb in and out of the cabs. The bus in the next lane of the bus station is a 1952 BMMO S13, with a dual-purpose Brush body working on the 517 route to Leamington. (Vectis)

361 (EKV 961)

Parked in the city centre in 1951 is 361 (EKV 961), a Brush-bodied Daimler CWA6 that had entered service in February 1945. The bus had been fitted with extra half-drop saloon windows and upholstered seating to replace the original wooden slatted seats, but is otherwise in its original condition, even to the extent of retaining the small original destination aperture. The bus is going on a journey to Stoke Aldermoor. During the Second World War, the Rootes No. 1 shadow factory was located in Stoke Aldermoor producing four-wheel drive scout cars, tank engines, lorry engines and aircraft engines. (D. R. Harvey Collection)

362 (EKV 962)

On a miserable day in February 1945, Coventry Transport's 362 (EKV 962) was photographed at the Brush factory in Loughborough for posterity. This was the first of the last pair of Brush-bodied Daimler CWA6s to be built for Coventry. Although painted in a red oxide and cream livery and still sporting wooden slatted seats, which would be replaced a few weeks later by the Corporation, the signs of Relaxed Utility bodies were beginning to be introduced. The half-drop saloon windows were staggered and, by the end of the year, Keresley Works had doubled them by fitting new sets directly opposite the originals. With the exception of the rear dome, which was still constructed on the lobster pattern of separate angled pieces of sheet metal, the early post-war Brush body evolved from this style. What is surprising is that the body pillars were so thin, perhaps reflecting the need to rebuild them, in this case by Bond in 1953. (Brush)

363 (EKV 963)

With its conductor propping up a passenger railing in Pool Meadow bus station, Roe-rebodied Daimler CWA6 363 (EKV 963) waits at the bus shelter for the 13 route to Willenhall. This bus originally had a Duple UH30/26R body and, as with this entire batch of ten buses, was delivered in August 1944. Unusually for the normally robust Duple war-time body, no fewer than twelve of them were chosen for rebodying by Roe as it was not deemed economical to repair them.

In 1958, 363 became the first of these rebodies to be taken out of service, whereupon it was renumbered 01 and converted to a tree lopper and sometime ceremonial bus by the removal of the top deck. In this guise it survived until 1967. To the rear is 149 (KVC 149), one of the 1952 Daimler CVD6s with Birmingham-styled MCCW H31/27R bodywork. (D. R. Harvey Collection)

365 (EKV 965)

Working on the 9 route to Earlsdon is 365 (EKV 965). This Duple-bodied Daimler CWA6 is standing on the east side of Broadgate in front of the long-lived temporary shops. Just visible is the fourteenth-century west window of the Holy Trinity church. Rebuilt by Nudd Brothers & Lockyer during 1951, the only remnants of the original body were the angle top at the rear of the driver's cab door and the raised bottom of the offside cab panelling, which lined up with the bottom of the windscreen rather than the waist rail level of the lower-saloon windows. This bus was fitted with experimental high-backed seats in the upper saloon that were unique to the rebuilt 365. (R. Marshall)

366 (EKV 966)

Above: On 30 August 1994, West Midlands Travel had an open day at Acocks Green Garage. Visiting preserved buses were allowed to operate on the 1 route from Acocks Green to Birmingham City Centre via Moseley. One of the visiting buses, which was a static exhibit, was Coventry Transport's 366 (EKV 966).

This Roe-rebodied Daimler CWA6 had been numbered 02 in the Coventry service fleet from 1959 to 1971. It had recently been repainted, but was not yet fitted with a full complement of seats since the bus had been used as a mobile workshop. Alongside it is former Birmingham City Transport 2489 (JOJ 489), owned by the author. The bus is a Crossley DD42/6 with a Crossley body dating from 1950, some of which were allocated to Acocks Green Garage when new. (D. R. Harvey)

367 (EKV 967)

Opposite above: Picking up passengers in Ford Street in front of the 1863 brick and stone dressed Municipal School of Art is 367 (EKV 967). Alongside the bus is Holy Trinity Church School, which continues to the right to form the corner of Ford Street and Hales Street. This Duple-bodied Daimler CWA6 is working on the 7 route to Allesley. This is the later Duple version of the 'relaxed' MoS Utility body with an extra pair of half drop saloon windows, glazed emergency exit in the upper saloon and the bottom of the cab side higher than the level of the lower saloon windows. (W. J. Haynes)

368 (EKV 968)

Opposite below: A pre-war Morris Eight enters Broadgate from the distant Trinity Street and passes the Utility bus shelters in front of Holy Trinity church as it moves out to pass the stationary Coventry Transport bus 368 (EKV 968), a Duple-bodied Daimler CWA6 delivered in August 1944. The bus is in original condition except for being repainted in full fleet livery and, while it was delivered with upholstered seats, it was still retaining its single aperture front destination blind and a single pair of half-drop windows in each saloon. The bus has retained its original military type, small diameter wartime headlights. (D. R. Harvey Collection)

369 (EKV 969)

369 (EKV 969) was one of twelve Daimler CWA6s to receive the attractively proportioned teak-framed Roe H31/25R bodies in 1951. By rebodying these 1944-vintage chassis, Coventry Transport virtually created a new bus; some chassis rebuilding had taken place prior to rebodying, thus creating virtually a post-war specification CVA6 model. 369 lasted as long as some of that model supplied to Coventry in the 194–1950 period and was not withdrawn until 1964. It is parked in the bus station alongside a portable Consul air raid shelter, which looks like a huge artillery shell. These could accommodate two people and give protection against shrapnel and falling masonry during an air raid. They were quite often used at railway and bus stations and provided shelter for bus staff after they had guided passengers to communal air raid shelters. (S. N. J. White)

370 (EKV 970)

Straddling the remains of the tram tracks, 370 (EKV 970) is parked on the cobbles in front of the tall entrance gates to the old Priestleys Bridge tram sheds. This area was by now at the edge of the Harnall Lane garage complex and was used for outdoor parking, with bus 76 (GKV 76), a 1949 Metro-Cammell-bodied Daimler CVA6, just visible. 370, a Daimler CWA6 with a Duple body, had been rebuilt by Nudd Brothers & Lockyer in 1951 and would be outlived by only a year by the distant 76. The Nudd rebuilds did not look as professionally finished as those undertaken by Bond with the rubber mounted windows, especially those side ones in the front dome that looked from certain angles like windows fitted to caravans. (M. Rooum)

371 (EKV 971)

Above: Standing in the wet-floored Sandy Lane Garage is 373 (EKV 971). This was a 1944 Daimler CWA6 that had been reseated in 1949 to the unusual H31/27R layout but, despite it being rebuilt at Keresley Works, the Duple bodywork was in such a poor state of repair that it was a prime candidate for rebodying. 371 was rebodied by Charles Roe in 1951 with their attractively designed teak-framed bodywork that incorporated the Roe patent staircase. This had two landings and was designed to prevent passengers falling down the length of the stairs. The curved staircase window on the offside was another identifier for a Roe-built body. 371 would remain in service until 1964. (D. R. Harvey Collection)

373 (FDU 373)

Above: Standing in Broadgate at the top of Trinity Street is newly rebodied 373 (FDU 373). A traffic inspector appears to have given last-minute instructions to the driver of this Daimler CWA6. The bus, dating from August 1945, originally had a Relaxed Utility body built by Duple. It is working on a Coventry City FC football special to Highfield Lane where, no doubt, many of the fans would have followed the advice of the advertisement on the side of the bus and be dragging away on a Capstan cigarette, which were extremely strong. Parked at the top of Trinity Street is Daimler CVA6 61 (GKV 61) with a Metro-Cammell body, which dates from 1949. (R. Marshall)

372 (EKV 972)

Opposite below: 372 was the last of the 1944 Daimler CWA6s delivered in August of that year and had a Duple HH30/26R body. This batch of later Duple wartime bodies, numbered 363–372, originally came in red oxide and cream livery and had cab side windows with a raised waistline to the depth of the windscreen. 372 was the only one of these ten to have continuous rain strips above the windows of both decks. Most of the other wartime buses only ever had guttering over the opening saloon windows. It is at the Tile Hill terminus in October 1951. 372 had been reseated in 1949 as a fifty-eight-seater with a H31/27R layout, which it retained after its body was rebuilt by Bond. (D. F. Parker)

375 (FDU 375)

Above left: Running empty to AWA works at Bagington along London Road, just beyond the box section railway bridge, is 375 (FDU 375), a Roe-rebodied Daimler CWA6. The driver has his right hand lazily out of the window while holding a cigarette, he can get away with it because the bus is empty (save for his conductor).

The Armstrong Whitworth Aircraft factory was set up to produce aircraft in the 1930s and produced the Whitley bomber, the Albemarle, which was a light bomber, and more than 1300 Avro Lancaster four-engined bombers under licence during the years of the Second World War. By the time 375 was on its way to the factory, AWA were producing several hundred Gloster Meteors, particularly the night-fighter versions. (P. Yeomans)

375 (FDU 375)

Below left: A Roe-rebodied Daimler CWA6 works on an outbound 18A service in about 1957 as a virtually new Standard 10 travels in the opposite direction. 375 (FDU 375) is in Sheriff Avenue with the late 1930s shops in Prior Deram Walk in the background. The bus had, a few minutes earlier, crossed the main A45 Fletchamstead Highway, having served the Standard Motor Works in Canley Road on its way into Coventry's western suburbia. 375 had been rebodied by Roe with a H31/25R layout body in 1951 and would be one of the last wartime Daimlers to remain in service, finally going in 1964. (C. W. Routh)

376 (FDU 376)

Above right: The AEC engine had obviously become hot as the bonnet side panel has been propped open in order to get some cooler air over the engine. In practice this made little difference, the only effect being that it made the smell of engine oil and leaking diesel more noticeable. 376 (FDU 376) is a Daimler CWA6, with a chassis dated to September 1945, and had its Duple body rebuilt by Bond in 1952. The sharper-shaped front-dome side windows and the square front windows were a distinguishing feature of the Bond reconstructions when compared to the Nudd rebuilds. 376 waits at the Broad Street bus stop in Fairfax Street near to the bus station on Tuesday 11 June 1963. (W. Ryan)

378 (FDU 378)

Below right: Parked with other withdrawn buses is 378 (FDU 378), a Duple-bodied Daimler CWA6 delivered in October 1945. This bus was extensively rebuilt by Bond of Wythenshawe in 1952. Alongside it is Weymann-bodied 342 (EKV 942), which was one of only two Coventry Transport wartime buses to be rebuilt by East Lancashire at Bridlington. The two East Lancs rebuilds (the other was 309) could be distinguished by the lack of beading below the windscreen on the cab apron. These two buses were withdrawn in 1963 and were awaiting collection by Milleons of Barnsley, who would break both of them up in the early part of 1964. (D. R. Harvey Collection)

383 (FDU 383)

Above: Before it was rebuilt by Bond in 1953, 383 (FDU 383) stands in Broadgate on 6 September 1951 before leaving for Cheylesmore on the 2 service. These last ten wartime buses, numbered 373–386, were Daimler CWA6Ds to wartime design that had a rather protracted delivery time, with the first eight delivered between August November 1945 and the last two not arriving until March 1946. Their Duple bodies were to the Relaxed wartime design, featuring curved rear domes, more opening windows in each saloon and twin destination boxes. They were delivered with upholstered maroon rexine seats in a red oxide and cream livery. (A. Cooper)

380 (FDU 380)

Opposite above: With its springs groaning under full load, 380 (FDU 380), a Bond-rebuilt Duple-bodied Daimler CWA6D, is overloaded with workers as it leaves one of Coventry's many car manufacturing factories on a works service back to the city centre. The body is almost down on to the wheel arches as the driver is about to haul his charge to the right. If the tyre pressures were inflated to the correct level and the steering box was well greased then this was quite manageable, if somewhat hard, work. If not, it was extremely hard work. (C. W. Routh)

382 (FDU 382)

Opposite below: Setting out from Armstrong Whitworth Aircraft factory at Baginton is 382 (FDU 382), a 1945-vintage Daimler CWA6 that was rebodied by Charles Roe in 1951 with a H31/25R seating layout. It is well-laden with workers and one wonders if the man in the gabardine mackintosh was able to find a seat. The last ten wartime Daimlers were classified CWA6D as they had a Daimler-built rear axle rather than the Kirkstall rear axle, and could be identified by having a flat-faced rear axle differential hub. 382 remained in service until 1963, whereupon it became Tuition Bus 04 for eleven months from February 1964. (Vectis)

383 (FDU 383)

Above: This is what rebuilding by Bond of Wythenshawe did to the original Duple-built structure of 383 (FDU 383). Parked at the 13A shelter in Pool Meadow bus station in about 1956, the bodywork on this Daimler CWA6D has been transformed and modernised, but it is debateable if it looks better than in its original condition. It must, however, have been more comfortable and less basic for the riding passengers. The advertisement on the side of the bus is for Guyvers of Greyfriars Street, who were Rover and Land Rover agents. (C. Carter)

384 (FDU 384)

Opposite above: The steps of Priory Row behind the bus lead away from the top of Trinity Street in front of the mock-Elizabethan premises of Timothy Whites chemists towards the genuine fifteenth-century timber-framed Lychgate Cottage buildings. 384 (FDU 384) was numerically the last of the twelve Daimler CWA6D to be rebodied with Roe fifty-six-seat bodies during 1951. It is working on the long 20 to Bedworth. The Roe bodies all replaced late wartime Duple Relaxed Utility bodies which, because of the unavoidable use of unseasoned ash used in their construction, were considered to be beyond reconstruction. Typical of the Roe designs coming out of their Crossgates factory from about 1948 until 1952, the bodies had deep lower-saloon windows that contrasted to the shallower upper-saloon windows. They all had the Roe safety staircase that made an incursion into the lower saloon, resulting in a much shorter fifth offside bay and the characteristic rounded staircase window. The were noticeably much than on those downstairs. The teak waist rail below the lower-saloon windows was always a Roe styling feature, as was the curved profile of the front elevation. (R. Marshall)

386 (FDU 386)

Opposite below: The last wartime bus was actually delivered in March 1946 and was also the last bus to be numbered in the original series as, two years after, the new post-war buses had fleet numbers beginning with '1'. 386 (FDU 386) was a Daimler CWA6D with a Relaxed Utility MoS-designed Duple H30/26R and is in the full early post-war Coventry Transport livery of maroon with three cream bands, plus cream painted upper-saloon guttering. Only this one and 385, also delivered in March 1945, arrived in full fleet livery. 386 is working on the 3 route to Stoke Aldermoor in 1949. (S. N. J. White)

Coventry Transport
Bus Fleet 1914–1946

Fleet No.	Regist. No.	Chassis	Chassis No.	Body	Seating	Modifications/ Notes	Year In	Year Out
1	DU 258	Maudslay 40hp	?	Brush	O18/16RO	Impressed WD 9/14.	3/14	9/14
2	DU 259	Maudslay 40hp	?	Brush	O18/16RO	Impressed WD 9/14.	3/14	9/14
3	DU 260	Maudslay 40hp	?	Brush	O18/16RO	Impressed WD 9/14.	3/14	9/14
4	DU 261	Maudslay 40hp	?	Brush	O18/16RO	Impressed WD 9/14.	3/14	9/14
5	DU 262	Maudslay 40hp	?	Brush	O18/16RO	Impressed WD 9/14.	3/14	9/14
6	DU 263	Maudslay 40hp	?	Brush	O18/16RO	Impressed WD 9/14.	3/14	9/14
1	HP 445	AEC YC	14921	Hora	B28R		11/1919	1930
2	HP 446	AEC YC	14920	Hora	B28R	Reseated B31R by 1931 and pneumatic tyres 1928.	11/1919	1933
3	HP 448	AEC YC	14917	Hora	B28R		11/1919	1930
4	HP 449	AEC YC	14916	Hora	B28R	Reseated B31R by 1931 and pneumatic tyres 1928.	11/1919	1934
5	HP 450	AEC YC	14915	Hora	B28R		11/1919	1931
6	HP 451	AEC YC	14919	Hora	B28R	Reseated B31R by 1931 and pneumatic tyres 1928.	11/1919	1932
7	HP 452	AEC YC	14918	Hora	B28R	Reseated B31R by 1931.	11/1919	1931
8	HP 447	Maudslay Subsidy A	3581	General Seat	B36R	Reseated B34R by 1931 and pneumatic tyres 1928.	2/1921	1934
9	HP 2182	Maudslay Subsidy A	3582	General Seat	B36R	Reseated B34R by 1931 and pneumatic tyres 1928.	2/1921	1934

Fleet No.	Regist. No.	Chassis	Chassis No.	Body	Seating	Modifications/ Notes	Year In	Year Out
10	HP 2183	Maudslay Subsidy A	3583	General Seat	B36R	Reseated B34R by 1931 and pneumatic tyres 1928.	2/1921	1934
11	HP 2184	Maudslay Subsidy A	3584	General Seat	B36R	Reseated B34R by 1931 and pneumatic tyres 1928.	2/1921	1934
12	HP 5744	Maudslay CP	3618	Hickman	FO58RO	Reseated FO56RO by 1927.	1923	1934
13	HP 9001	Maudslay CP	3642	Hickman	FO58RO	Reseated FO56RO by 1927.	1924	1934
14	HP 9009	Maudslay CP	3646	Hickman	FO58RO	Reseated FO56RO by 1927.	1924	1933
15	RW 1999	Maudslay CP	3707	Hickman	FO58RO	Reseated FO56RO by 1927.	1925	1934
16	RW 1998	Maudslay CP	3708	Hickman	FO58RO	Reseated FO56RO by 1927.	1925	1934
17	RW 5000	Maudslay CP	3744	Hickman	H54RO	Reseated H52RO by 1927.	1925	1934
18	RW 5001	Maudslay CP	3745	Hickman	H54RO	Reseated H52RO by 1927.	1925	1934
19	RW 5119	Maudslay CP	3785	Hickman	H54RO	Reseated H52RO by 1927.	1925	1934
20	WK 500	Maudslay ML4A	4061	Hickman	B26D		3/1927	1937
21	WK 501	Maudslay ML4A	4060	Hickman	B26D		3/1927	1938
22	WK 502	Maudslay ML4A	4062	Hickman	B26D		3/1927	1938
23	WK 3101	Maudslay ML4A	4165	Hickman	B26D		7/1927	1938
24	WK 3102	Maudslay ML4A	4166	Hickman	B26D		7/1927	1935
25	WK 3103	Maudslay ML4A	4167	Hickman	B26D		7/1927	1938
26	WK 6601	Maudslay ML4A	4353	Hickman	B26D		6/1928	1938
27	WK 6602	Maudslay ML4A	4354	Hickman	B26D		6/1928	1935
28	WK 6603	Maudslay ML4A	4356	Hickman	B26D		6/1928	1938

Fleet No.	Regist. No.	Chassis	Chassis No.	Body	Seating	Modifications/ Notes	Year In	Year Out
29	WK 6604	Maudslay ML4A	4355	Hickman	B26D		6/1928	1938
30	WK 6605	Maudslay ML4A	4357	Hickman	B26D		6/1928	1935
31	WK 7501	Maudslay ML4A	4450	Hickman	B26D		8/1928	1935
32	WK 7502	Maudslay ML4A	4451	Hickman	B26D		8/1928	1935
33	WK 7503	Maudslay ML4A	4452	Hickman	B26D		9/1928	1938
34	VC 1784	Maudslay ML4C	4722	Hickman	B26D		9/1929	1935
35	VC 1785	Maudslay ML4C	4723	Hickman	B26D		9/1929	1935
36	WK 7686	Maudslay CPL2	4435	Vickers	H24/24R		10/1928	1936
37	WK 7687	Maudslay CPL2	4436	Vickers	H24/24R		10/1928	1936
38	WK 7688	Maudslay CPL2	4437	Vickers	H24/24R		10/1928	1936
39	WK 7689	Maudslay CPL2	4438	Vickers	H24/24R		10/1928	1936
40	WK 8765	Maudslay Magna ML7 six-wheel	4439	Brush	FH33/27R		1/1929	1936
41	VC 2632	Maudslay Magna ML7 six-wheel	4780	Brush	H33/27R		12/1929	1938
42	VC 2633	Maudslay Magna ML7 six-wheel	4781	Brush	H33/27R		12/1929	1938
43	VC 5217	Maudslay Magna ML7 six-wheel	4884	Brush	H33/27R		6/1930	1939
44	VC 5218	Maudslay Magna ML7 six-wheel	4885	Brush	H33/27R		6/1930	1938
45	VC 5219	Maudslay Magna ML7 six-wheel	4886	Brush	H33/27R		6/1930	1938

Fleet No.	Regist. No.	Chassis	Chassis No.	Body	Seating	Modifications/ Notes	Year In	Year Out
46	VC 5220	Maudslay Magna ML7 six-wheel	4887	Brush	H33/27R		6/1930	1939
47	VC 1057	Daimler CF6	7155S	Brush	B26D	Demonstrator from 8/29. Purchased 8/1930.	1929	1947
48	VC 6515	Maudslay Magna ML7 six-wheel	4913	Brush	H33/27R		12/1930	1939
49	VC 6516	Maudslay Magna ML7 six-wheel	4909	Brush	H33/27R		12/1930	1939
50	VC 6517	Maudslay Magna ML7 six-wheel	4910	Brush	H33/27R		112/930	1939
51	VC 6518	Maudslay Magna ML7 six-wheel	4915	Brush	H33/27R		12/1930	1939
52	VC 6519	Maudslay Magna ML7 six-wheel	4914	Brush	H33/27R		12/1930	1938
53	VC 6520	Maudslay Magna ML7 six-wheel	4916	Brush	H33/27R		12/1930	1939
54	VC 6000	Dennis EV	17896	Brush	B32D		10/1930	1935
55	VC 9664	Maudslay Magna ML7 six-wheel	5009	Brush	H33/27R		10/1931	1939
56	VC 9665	Maudslay Magna ML7 six-wheel	5010	Brush	H33/27R		10/1931	1939
57	VC 9666	Maudslay Magna ML7 six-wheel	5011	Brush	H33/27R		10/1931	1939
58	VC 9667	Maudslay Magna ML7 six-wheel	5012	Brush	H33/27R		10/1931	1939

Fleet No.	Regist. No.	Chassis	Chassis No.	Body	Seating	Modifications/ Notes	Year In	Year Out
59	KV 721	Maudslay Magna ML7 four-wheel	5042	Brush	H26/24R		3/1932	1945
60	KV 722	Maudslay Magna ML7 four-wheel	5043	Brush	H26/24R		3/1932	1945
61	KV 723	Maudslay Magna ML7 four-wheel	5044	Brush	H26/24R		3/1932	1946
62	KV 724	Dennis Lance II	126037	Brush	H26/24R		3/1932	1943
63	KV 725	Dennis Lance II	126044	Brush	H26/24R		3/1932	1944
64	KV 726	Dennis 30 cwt	56581	Brush	B14F		3/1932	1936
65	KV 727	Dennis 30 cwt	56582	Brush	B14F		3/1932	1936
6##2 66	KV 64	Daimler CP6	9074	Weymann	H24/24R	Ex-demo to Ashton U L.	12/31	1949
100	VC 7519	Daimler CH6	9030	Buckingham	H26/24R	Ex-demo to Birmingham	1/1931	1938
101	KV 7101	Daimler CP6	9156	Brush	H26/24R	Reseated H27/26R 1939 Rebuilt Coventry Steel Caravans *c.* 1944	1/1934	1948
102	KV 7102	Daimler CP6	9154	Brush	H26/24R	Reseated H27/26R 1939 Rebuilt Coventry Steel Caravans *c.*1944	1/1934	1948
103	KV 7103	Daimler CP6	9155	Brush	H26/24R	Reseated H27/26R 1939 Rebuilt Coventry Steel Caravans *c.*1944	1/1934	1948
104	KV 7104	Daimler CP6	9172	Brush	H26/24R	Reseated H27/26R 1939 Rebuilt Coventry Steel Caravans *c.*1944	1/1934	1948
105	KV 7105	Daimler CP6	9173	Brush	H26/24R	Reseated H27/26R 1939 Rebuilt Coventry Steel Caravans *c.*1944	1/1934	1948

Fleet No.	Regist. No.	Chassis	Chassis No.	Body	Seating	Modifications/ Notes	Year In	Year Out
106	KV 7106	Daimler CP6	9174	Brush	H26/24R	Reseated H27/26R 1939 Rebuilt Coventry Steel Caravans *c.* 1944.	1/1934	1948
107	KV 7107	Daimler CP6	9147	Brush	H26/24R	Reseated H27/26R 1939 Rebuilt Coventry Steel Caravans *c.* 1944.	1/1934	1948
108 408	KV 7108	Daimler CP6	9157	Brush	H26/24R	Reseated H27/26R 1939. Rebodied Brush H31/29R, 5/42. To COG5 1945.	1/1934	1952
109	KV 7109	Daimler CP6	9134	Brush	H26/24R	Reseated H27/26R 1939 Rebuilt Coventry Steel Caravans *c.* 1944.	2/1934	1948
110	KV 7110	Daimler CP6	9176	Brush	H26/24R	Reseated H27/26R 1939 Rebuilt Coventry Steel Caravans *c.* 1944.	2/1934	1947
111	KV 7111	Daimler CP6	9171	Brush	H26/24R	Reseated H27/26R 1939 Rebuilt Coventry Steel Caravans *c.* 1944.	2/1934	1948
112	KV 7112	Daimler CP6	9179	Brush	H26/24R	Reseated H27/26R 1939 Rebuilt Coventry Steel Caravans *c.* 1944.	2/1934	1948
113	KV 7113	Daimler CP6	9178	Brush	H26/24R	Reseated H27/26R 1939 Rebuilt Coventry Steel Caravans *c.* 1944.	2/1934	1945
114	KV 7114	Daimler CP6	9175	Brush	H26/24R	Reseated H27/26R 1939 Rebuilt Coventry Steel Caravans *c.* 1944.	2/1934	1948
115	KV 7115	Daimler CP6	9132	Brush	H26/24R	Reseated H27/26R 1939 Rebuilt Coventry Steel Caravans *c.* 1944.	2/1934	1948

Fleet No.	Regist. No.	Chassis	Chassis No.	Body	Seating	Modifications/ Notes	Year In	Year Out
116	KV 7116	Daimler CP6	9177	Brush	H26/24R	Reseated H27/26R 1939 Rebuilt Coventry Steel Caravans *c.* 1944.	2/1934	1948
117 417	KV 9117	Daimler COA6	9222	MCCW	H26/24R	First Coventry metal framed body. Reseated H27/26R 1939.	11/1934	1951
118 418	KV 9118	Daimler COA6	9196	MCCW	H26/24R	Reseated H27/26R 1939.	11/1934	1948
119 419	KV 9119	Daimler COA6	9221	MCCW	H26/24R	Reseated H27/26R 1939.	11/1934	1951
120	KV 9120	Daimler CP6	9218	Brush	H26/24R	Reseated H27/26R 1939. Rebuilt Coventry Steel Caravans *c.* 1944.	11/1934	1948
121	KV 9121	Daimler CP6	9219	Brush	H26/24R	Reseated H27/26R 1939. Rebuilt Coventry Steel Caravans *c.* 1944.	11/1934	1945
122	KV 9122	Daimler CP6	9220	Brush	H26/24R	Last composite body supplied to Coventry. Reseated H27/26R 1939. Destroyed by enemy action 14.11.1940.	11/1934	1940
10	VC 5615	Dennis GL	70648	Brush	B20F	Ex Duckham, Coventry 1934.	7/1930	1937
123 423	AVC 123	Daimler COA6	9504	MCCW	H26/24R	Reseated H27/26R 1939.	10/1935	1952
124 424	AVC 124	Daimler COA6	9497	MCCW	H26/24R	Reseated H27/26R 1939.	10/1935	1952
125	AVC 125	Daimler COA6	9507	MCCW	H26/24R	Reseated H27/26R 1939.	10/1935	1949
126	AVC 126	Daimler COA6	9502	MCCW	H26/24R	Reseated H27/26R 1939. Chassis reassembled from parts of 128, 128 and 167. Rebodied Brush H31/29R 5/42.	10/1935	1949

Fleet No.	Regist. No.	Chassis	Chassis No.	Body	Seating	Modifications/ Notes	Year In	Year Out
127 427	AVC 127	Daimler COA6	9499	MCCW	H26/24R	Reseated H27/26R 1939.	10/1935	1952
128	AVC 128	Daimler COA6	9503	MCCW	H26/24R	Reseated H27/26R 1939. Destroyed 1940.	10/1935	1941
129	AVC 129	Daimler COA6	9501	MCCW	H26/24R	Reseated H27/26R 1939. Rebodied Brush H31/29R 5/42.	10/1935	1949
130	AVC 130	Daimler COA6	9500	MCCW	H26/24R	Reseated H27/26R 1939.	10/1935	1949
131 431	AVC 131	Daimler COA6	9505	MCCW	H26/24R	Reseated H27/26R 1939.	11/1935	1952
132	AVC 132	Daimler COA6	9506	MCCW	H26/24R	Reseated H27/26R 1939.	12/1935	1950
133	AVC 133	Daimler COA6	9496	MCCW	H26/24R	Reseated H27/26R 1939.	10/1935	1950
134	AVC 134	Daimler COA6	0498	MCCW	H26/24R	Reseated H27/26R 1939.	11/1935	1951
135	AVC 135	Daimler COA6	9493	MCCW	H26/24R	Reseated H27/26R 1939.	10/1935	1950
136 436	AVC 136	Daimler COA6	9509	MCCW	H26/24R	Reseated H27/26R 1939.	11/1935	1952
137	AVC 137	Daimler COA6	9494	MCCW	H26/24R	Reseated H27/26R 1939.	10/1935	1950
138	AVC 138	Daimler COA6	9510	MCCW	H26/24R	Reseated H27/26R 1939.	11/1935	1951
139	AVC 139	Daimler COA6	9508	MCCW	H26/24R	Reseated H27/26R 1939.	11/1935	1949
140	AVC 140	Daimler COA6	9495	MCCW	H26/24R	Reseated H27/26R 1939.	10/1935	1949
141	AVC 141	Daimler COA6	9511	MCCW	H26/24R	Reseated H27/26R 1939.	11/1935	1949
142	AVC 142	Daimler COA6	9512	MCCW	H26/24R	Reseated H27/26R 1939.	12/1935	1949
143	BDU 143	Leyland Cub IKPO2	4421	Brush	B20F		1936	1938
144	BDU 144	Leyland Cub IKPO2	4422	Brush	B20F		1936	1938
145	BHP 145	Leyland Cub IKPO2	4395	Brush	B20F		1936	1938
146	BHP 146	Daimler COG5	8164	MCCW	B34F	To Birmingham CT specification.	3/1936	1949

Fleet No.	Regist. No.	Chassis	Chassis No.	Body	Seating	Modifications/ Notes	Year In	Year Out
147	BWK 147	Daimler COA6	9695	Brush	H29/26R		8/1936	1949
148	BWK 148	Daimler COA6	9696	Brush	H29/26R		9/1936	1952
149	BWK 149	Daimler COA6	9697	Brush	H29/26R		9/1936	1951
150	BWK 150	Daimler COA6	9698	Brush	H29/26R		9/1936	1949
151	BWK 151	Daimler COA6	9699	Brush	H29/26R		9/1936	1949
152	BWK 152	Daimler COA6	9700	Brush	H29/26R		9/1936	1951
153	BWK 153	Daimler COA6	9701	Brush	H29/26R	Re No. 453, 1952.	9/1936	1952
154	BWK 154	Daimler COA6	9702	Brush	H29/26R		9/1936	1947
155	BWK 155	Daimler COA6	9703	Brush	H29/26R	Rebodied Roe H31/26R 4/49. Re No. 455, 1952.	9/1936	1958
156	BWK 156	Daimler COA6	9704	Brush	H29/26R		10/1936	1950
157	BWK 157	Daimler COA6	9705	Brush	H29/26R		9/1936	1951
158	BWK 158	Daimler COA6	9706	Brush	H29/26R		9/1936	1949
159	BWK 159	Daimler COA6	9707	Brush	H29/26R		9/1936	1949
160	BWK 160	Daimler COA6	9708	Brush	H29/26R	Flared lower skirt panels.	9/1936	1949
161	BWK 161	Daimler COA6	9709	Brush	H29/26R	Rebodied Roe H31/26R 4/49. Re No. 461, 1952.	9/1936	1958
162	BKV 162	Daimler COA6	9837	Brush	H29/26R		2/1937	1949
163	BKV 163	Daimler COA6	9836	Brush	H29/26R		1/1937	1950
164	BKV 164	Daimler COA6	9841	Brush	H29/26R	Rebodied Brush H31/29R 6/42.	1/1937	1949
165	BKV 165	Daimler COA6	9839	Brush	H29/26R		1/1937	1951
166	BKV 166	Daimler COA6	9838	Brush	H29/26R		1/1937	1950

Fleet No.	Regist. No.	Chassis	Chassis No.	Body	Seating	Modifications/ Notes	Year In	Year Out
167	BKV 167	Daimler COA6	9840	Brush	H29/26R	Destroyed 8.4.41.	2/1937	1941
168	BKV 168	Daimler COA6	9845	Brush	H29/26R		1/1937	1951
169	BKV 169	Daimler COA6	9842	Brush	H29/26R		2/1937	1951
170	BKV 170	Daimler COA6	9844	Brush	H29/26R	Re No. 470, 1955.	2/1937	1956
171	BKV 171	Daimler COA6	9847	Brush	H29/26R		2/1937	1952
172	BKV 172	Daimler COA6	9846	Brush	H29/26R		2/1937	1952
173	BKV 173	Daimler COA6	9843	Brush	H29/26R	Rebodied Roe H31/26R 4/49. Re No. 473, 1955.	2/1937	1958
174	AMV 433	AEC Q##0761	0761016	Park Royal	H31/29F	On loan 1937.	1933	1938
176	CMF 843	AEC Renown 0664	0664254	Weymann	B43F	On loan 1937.	1935	1937
	AML272	AEC Regent 0661	0661 2267	Park Royal	L27/27R	On loan 1937	1933	1937
	JR 1573	Daimler COG5	9133	?	H24/24R	On loan 1937.	2/1934	1937
174	CWK 174	Daimler COG5/40	8337	Park Royal	B38F	Cream livery.	12/1938	1949
175	CWK 175	Daimler COG5/40	8338	Park Royal	B38F	Cream livery To B32F and perimeter 1943.	10/1938	1949
176	CWK 176	Daimler COG5/40	8339	Park Royal	B38F		1/1938	1949
177	CWK 177	Daimler COG5/40	8340	Park Royal	B38F		1/1938	1949
178	CWK 178	Daimler COG5/40	8341	Park Royal	B38F		1/1938	1949
179	CWK 179	Daimler COA6	10243	Park Royal	H29/26R		12/1937	1950
180	CWK 180	Daimler COA6	10245	Park Royal	H29/26R		12/1937	1950
181	CWK 181	Daimler COA6	10244	Park Royal	H29/26R		12/1937	1952
182	CWK 182	Daimler COA6	10246	Brush	H29/26R		12/1937	1951

Fleet No.	Regist. No.	Chassis	Chassis No.	Body	Seating	Modifications/ Notes	Year In	Year Out
183	CWK 183	Daimler COA6	10248	Brush	H29/26R	Destroyed by enemy action 14.11.1940.	12/1937	1940
184	CWK 184	Daimler COA6	10249	Brush	H29/26R		12/1937	1949
185	CWK 185	Daimler COA6	10247	Brush	H29/26R		1/1938	1951
186	CWK 186	Daimler COA6	10250	Brush	H29/26R		1/1938	1953
187	CWK 187	Daimler COA6	10251	Brush	H29/26R	Re No. 487, 1955.	1/1938	1956
188	CWK 188	Daimler COA6	10253	Brush	H29/26R	New Brush roof 9/42.	1/1938	1950
189	CWK 189	Daimler COA6	10254	Brush	H29/26R		1/1938	1950
190	CWK 190	Daimler COA6	10256	Brush	H29/26R		1/1938	1950
191	CWK 191	Daimler COA6	10255	Brush	H29/26R		1/1938	1953
192	CWK 192	Daimler COA6	10252	Brush	H29/26R		1/1938	1955
193	CWK 193	Daimler COA6	10259	Brush	H29/26R		1/1938	1953
194	CWK 194	Daimler COA6	10261	Brush	H29/26R		2/1938	1949
195	CWK 195	Daimler COA6	10263	Brush	H29/26R		2/1938	1953
196	CWK 196	Daimler COA6	10260	Brush	H29/26R		2/1938	1956
197	CWK 197	Daimler COA6	10258	Brush	H29/26R		2/1938	1949
198	CWK 198	Daimler COA6	10264	Brush	H29/26R		2/1938	1955
199	CWK 199	Daimler COA6	10262	Brush	H29/26R	Rebodied Roe H31/26R 4/49. Re No. 499, 1956.	2/1938	1958
200	CWK 200	Daimler COA6	10257	Brush	H29/26R		2/1938	1955
201	CWK 201	Daimler COA6	10268	Brush	H29/26R	Rebodied Roe H31/26R 4/49. Re No. 401, 1956.	3/1938	1958
202	CWK 202	Daimler COA6	10266	Brush	H29/26R		3/1938	1950

Fleet No.	Regist. No.	Chassis	Chassis No.	Body	Seating	Modifications/ Notes	Year In	Year Out
203	CWK 203	Daimler COA6	10267	Brush	H29/26R	1937 CMS exhibit.	12/1937	1950
204	CWK 204	Daimler COA6	10265	Brush	H29/26R		3/1938	1950
205	CWK 205	Daimler COA6	10269	Brush	H29/26R	Reversed cream livery. Known as 'The White Lady'.	4/1938	1955
206	DHP 206	Daimler COG5/40	8393	Park Royal	B38F		4/1938	1949
207	DHP 207	Daimler COG5/40	8394	Park Royal	B38F		4/1938	1949
208	DHP 208	Daimler COG5/40	8395	Park Royal	B38F	To B32F and perimeter 7/1942–12/1945.	4/1938	1949
209	DWK 209	Daimler COG5/40	8429	Park Royal	B38F		6/1938	1949
210	DWK 210	Daimler COG5/40	8430	Park Royal	B38F	To B32F and perimeter 7/1942.	6/1938	1949
211	DWK 211	Daimler COG5/40	8431	Park Royal	B38F		6/1938	1949
212	DKV 212	Daimler COA6	10685	MCCW	H30/26R		4/1939	1956
213	DKV 213	Daimler COA6	10678	MCCW	H30/26R	Reseated 1954 with seats from three 1949 Daimler CVD6s.	4/1939	1955
214	DKV 214	Daimler COA6	10679	MCCW	H30/26R	New Brush roof 1941.	4/1939	1952
215	DKV 215	Daimler COA6	10681	MCCW	H30/26R		4/1939	1956
216	DKV 216	Daimler COA6	10687	MCCW	H30/26R		4/1939	1955
217	DKV 217	Daimler COA6	10682	MCCW	H30/26R	New Brush roof 1941.	5/1939	1955
218	DKV 218	Daimler COA6	10684	MCCW	H30/26R		5/1939	1956
219	DKV 219	Daimler COA6	10688	MCCW	H30/26R	New Brush roof 1941.	5/1939	1956
220	DKV 220	Daimler COA6	10683	MCCW	H30/26R		5/1939	1956
221	DKV 221	Daimler COA6	10686	MCCW	H30/26R		5/1939	1956
222	DKV 222	Daimler COA6	10680	MCCW	H30/26R		5/1939	1953

Fleet No.	Regist. No.	Chassis	Chassis No.	Body	Seating	Modifications/ Notes	Year In	Year Out
223	DKV 223	Daimler COA6	10689	Massey	H30/26R	1st Massey metal-framed.	5/1939	1953
224	DKV 224	Daimler COA6	10690	Brush	H29/26R		3/1939	1956
225	DKV 225	Daimler COA6	10691	Brush	H29/26R		3/1939	1956
226	DKV 226	Daimler COA6	10692	Brush	H29/26R		3/1939	1956
227	DKV 227	Daimler COA6	10693	Brush	H29/26R		3/1939	1953
228	DKV 228	Daimler COA6	10694	Brush	H29/26R		4/1939	1953
229	DKV 229	Daimler COA6	10695	Brush	H29/26R		3/1939	1953
230	EHP 230	Daimler COG5/60	10827	Brush	H29/31R		8/1939	1952
231	EHP 231	Daimler COG5/60	10828	Brush	H29/31R	New Brush roof 1941.	8/1939	1952
232	EHP 232	Daimler COG5/60	10829	Brush	H29/31R		7/1939	1952
233	EHP 233	Daimler COG5/60	10830	Brush	H29/31R		8/1939	1953
234	EHP 234	Daimler COA6	10825	MCCW	H31/29R	New Brush roof 1941.	11/1939	1950
235	EHP 235	Daimler COA6	10824	MCCW	H31/29R		11/1939	1952
236	EHP 236	Daimler COA6	10823	MCCW	H31/29R		12/1939	1956
237	EHP 237	Daimler COA6	10826	MCCW	H31/29R		12/1939	1950
238	EWK 238	Daimler COG5/60	11043	Brush	H29/31R		11/1939	1952
239	EWK 239	Daimler COG5/60	11044	Brush	H29/31R		12/1939	1950
240	EWK 240	Daimler COG5/60	11045	Brush	H29/31R	Body destroyed by enemy action 14/11/1940. Rebodied Brush UH 31/29R, 11/42. Converted to COD6 4/45.	11/1939	1955
241	EWK 241	Daimler COG5/60	11046	Brush	H29/31R		11/1939	1952

Fleet No.	Regist. No.	Chassis	Chassis No.	Body	Seating	Modifications/ Notes	Year In	Year Out
4(264)	CP 8010 Ex-Halifax Corp 54	AEC Regent 661	661040	Hoyal	H26/24RO	Rebodied Brush UH30/26R, -/43.	1929	1948
5(265)	CP 8011 Ex-Halifax Corp 55	AEC Regent 661	661038	Hoyal	H26/24RO	Rebodied Brush UH30/26R, -/43.	1929	1948
7(267)	CP 9070 Ex-Halifax JOC 114	AEC Regent 661	6611027	Hoyal	H26/24RO	Rebuilt by Coventry Steel Caravans -/43.	1931	1948
1	CP 9077 Ex-Halifax JOC 107	AEC Regent 661	6611016	Hoyal	H26/24RO		1931	1943
242	EVC 242	Daimler COG5/40	8556	Park Royal	B38F		6/1940	1949
243	EVC 243	Daimler COG5/40	8557	Park Royal	B38F		6/1940	1949
244	EVC 244	Daimler COG5/40	8558	Park Royal	B38F	Preserved.	6/1940	1949
245	EVC 245	Daimler COG5/60	11084	Brush	H29/31R	Intended for 1939 CMS.	12/1939	1952
246	EVC 246	Daimler COA6	11083	MCCW	H31/29R	Intended for 1939 CMS.	1/1940	1956
247	EVC 247	Daimler COG5/60	11119	Brush	H29/31R		5/1940	1952
248	EVC 248	Daimler COG5/60	11120	Brush	H29/31R		5/1940	1952
249	EVC 249	Daimler COG5/60	11128	Brush	H29/31R		11/1940	1951
250	EVC 250	Daimler COG5/60	11122	Brush	H29/31R		6/1940	1952
251	EVC 251	Daimler COG5/60	11123	Brush	H29/31R		6/1940	1952
252	EVC 252	Daimler COG5/60	11124	Brush	H29/31R		10/1940	1953
253	EVC 253	Daimler COG5/60	11125	Brush	H29/31R	Converted to COD6, 4/45.	10/1940	1952
254	EVC 254	Daimler COG5/60	11126	Brush	H29/31R	Rebodied Brush H29/31R, 6/42.	8/1940	1952
255	EVC 255	Daimler COG5/60	11127	Brush	H29/31R		8/1940	1952

Fleet No.	Regist. No.	Chassis	Chassis No.	Body	Seating	Modifications/ Notes	Year In	Year Out
256	EVC 256	Daimler COG5/60	11121	Brush	H29/31R	Converted to COD6, 4/45.	11/1940	1956
257	EVC 257	Daimler COG5/60	11129	Brush	H29/31R	Converted to COD6, 7/45.	10/1940	1957
258	EVC 258	Daimler COG5/60	11130	Brush	H29/31R	Rebodied Brush H29/31R, 6/42.	10/1940	1952
2	UJ 4901 Ex-Whittle, Highley	Leyland Cub SKP3	3280	Burlingham	C26R	Ex-Rover Co, Solihull 12/41.	1935	1945
259	EVC 259	AEC Regent 0661	0661 7214	Brush	H31/29R	'Unfrozen' chassis. Seven other chassis and bodies were built but diverted, six to BMMO and one to K-U-Hull CT.	1/1942	1958
260	EVC 260	AEC Regent 0661	0661 7215	Brush	H31/29R	'Unfrozen' chassis.	2/1942	1958
261	EVC 261	AEC Regent 0661	0661 7197	Brush	H31/29R	'Unfrozen' chassis.	2/1942	1958
9	WJ 517	Leyland Tiger TS3 Ex Sheffield CT 117	61762	Leyland	B30R	Acquired 1942.	1931	1945
10	WJ 519	Leyland Tiger TS3 Ex Sheffield CT 119	61764	Leyland	B30R	Acquired 1942.	1931	1945
11 263	WJ 520	Leyland Tiger TS3 Ex Sheffield CT 120	61765	Duple (1937)	C32F	Acquired 1942.	1931	1948
284	EKV 284	Bristol K5G	57052	Brush	UH30/26R	Reb Nudd Bros & Lockyer, 1951.	4/1942	1958
285	EKV 285	Guy Arab I 5LW	FD25453	Brush	UH29/27R	Reb Nudd Bros & Lockyer, 1951.	9/1942	1959
286	EKV 286	Guy Arab I 5LW	FD25460	Brush	UH29/27R	Reb Bond, Wythenshawe 1953.	9/1942	1958

Fleet No.	Regist. No.	Chassis	Chassis No.	Body	Seating	Modifications/ Notes	Year In	Year Out
287	EKV 287	Guy Arab I 5LW	FD25466	Brush	UH29/27R	Reb Nudd Bros & Lockyer, 1951.	9/1942	1959
288	EKV 288	Guy Arab I 5LW	FD25469	Brush	UH29/27R	Reb Bond, Wythenshawe 1953.	9/1942	1959
289	EKV 289	Guy Arab I 5LW	FD25480	Brush	UH29/27R	Reb Bond, Wythenshawe 1953.	9/1942	1958
290	EKV 290	Bedford OWB	8828	Roe	UB32F		9/1942	1948
291	EKV 291	Bedford OWB	8898	Roe	UB32F		9/1942	1948
292	EKV 292	Bedford OWB	8731	Roe	UB32F		10/1942	1948
293	EKV 293	Bedford OWB	9108	Roe	UB32F		9/1942	1948
294	EKV 294	Bedford OWB	8787	Roe	UB32F		9/1942	1948
295	EKV 295	Bedford OWB	9005	Roe	UB32F		9/1942	1948
296	EKV 296	Bedford OWB	9163	Roe	UB32F		10/1942	1948
297	EKV 297	Bedford OWB	9140	Roe	UB32F		9/1942	1948
298	EKV 298	Bedford OWB	9224	Roe	UB32F		9/1942	1948
299	EKV 299	Leyland Titan TD7	307052	NCME	UL27/26R	To Middlesbrough 11. Exchanged, ex-works for 330, (EKV 930).	11/1942	5/43
300	EKV 300	Guy Arab I 5LW	FD25689	Massey	UH30/26R	Reb Nudd Bros & Lockyer, 1951.	11/1942	1959
301	EKV 301	Guy Arab I 5LW	FD25694	Massey	UH30/26R	Reb Bond, Wythenshawe 1953.	11/1942	1958
302	EKV 302	Guy Arab I 5LW	FD25668	Weymann/ MCTD style	H30/26R	Manchester Streamline-style.	2/1943	1959
303	EKV 303	Guy Arab I 5LW	FD25719	Weymann/ MCTD style	H30/26R	Manchester Streamline.	4/1943	1961
304	EKV 304	Guy Arab I 5LW	FD25723	Weymann/ MCTD style	H30/26R	Manchester Streamline.	4/1943	1958

Fleet No.	Regist. No.	Chassis	Chassis No.	Body	Seating	Modifications/ Notes	Year In	Year Out
305	EKV 305	Guy Arab I 5LW	FD25812	Weymann/ MCTD style	H30/26R	Manchester Streamline.	3/1943	1959
306	EKV 306	Guy Arab I 5LW	FD25674	Weymann	UH30/26R	Reb Nudd Bros & Lockyer, 1951.	1/1943	1958
307	EKV 307	Guy Arab I 5LW	FD25678	Weymann	UH30/26R	Reb Bond, Wythenshawe 1953.	1/1943	1958
308	EKV 308	Guy Arab I 5LW	FD25679	Weymann	UH30/26R	Reb CCT 1951 and again 1955.	1/1943	1961
309	EKV 709	Guy Arab I 5LW	FD25695	Weymann	UH30/26R	Reb East Lancs, Bridlington 1952.	1/1943	1958
310	EKV 710	Guy Arab I 5LW	FD25677	Park Royal	UH30/26R	Reb Nudd Bros & Lockyer, 1951.	1/1943	1959
311	EKV 711	Guy Arab I 5LW	FD25680	Park Royal	UH30/26R	Reb Nudd Bros & Lockyer, 1951.	1/1943	1959
312	EKV 712	Guy Arab I 5LW	FD25696	Park Royal	UH30/26R	Reb Nudd Bros & Lockyer, 1951.	1/1943	1958
313	EKV 713	Guy Arab I 5LW	FD25697	Park Royal	UH30/26R	Reb Bond, Wythenshawe 1952.	1/1943	1958
314	EKV 714	Guy Arab I 5LW	FD25699	Park Royal	UH30/26R	Reb Nudd Bros & Lockyer, 1951.	1/1943	1961
315	EKV 715	Guy Arab I 5LW	FD25700	Park Royal	UH30/26R	Reb Nudd Bros & Lockyer, 1951.	1/1943	1958
316 (416)	EKV 816	Daimler CWG5	11329	Duple	UH30/26R	Reb Nudd Bros & Lockyer, 1951.	3/1943	1964
317	EKV 817	Daimler CWG5	11341	Duple	UH30/26R	Reb Bond, Wythenshawe 1953.	4/1943	1958
318	EKV 818	Daimler CWG5	11342	Duple	UH30/26R	Reb Bond, Wythenshawe 1953.	4/1943	1958
319 (419)	EKV 819	Daimler CWG5	11355	Duple	UH30/26R	Reb Nudd Bros & Lockyer, 1951.	5/1943	1963
320	EKV 820	Daimler CWG5	11397	Duple	UH30/26R	Reb Bond, Wythenshawe 1953.	7/1943	1958

Fleet No.	Regist. No.	Chassis	Chassis No.	Body	Seating	Modifications/ Notes	Year In	Year Out
321 (421)	EKV 821	Daimler CWG5	11400	Duple	UH30/26R	Reb CCT 1949.	7/1943	1963
322 (422)	EKV 822	Daimler CWG5	11335	Duple	UH30/26R	Reb CCT 1951.	3/1943	1964
323	EKV 823	Guy Arab II 5LW	FD25954	Weymann	UH30/26R	Reb Nudd Bros & Lockyer, 1950.	5/1943	1958
324	EKV 824	Guy Arab II 5LW	FD25956	Weymann	UH30/26R	Reb CCT 1950.	6/1943	1958
325	EKV 825	Guy Arab II 5LW	FD25968	Weymann	UH30/26R	Reb Nudd Bros & Lockyer, 1951.	6/1943	1961
326	EKV 826	Guy Arab II 5LW	FD25971	Weymann	UH30/26R	Reb Nudd Bros & Lockyer, 1951.	6/1943	1958
327	EKV 827	Guy Arab II 5LW	FD26049	Weymann	UH30/26R	Reb Nudd Bros & Lockyer, 1951.	7/1943	1961
328	EKV 828	Guy Arab II 5LW	FD26056	Weymann	UH30/26R	Reb Nudd Bros & Lockyer, 1951.	7/1943	1959
329	EKV 829	Guy Arab II 5LW	FD26057	Weymann	UH30/26R	Reb Bond, Wythenshawe 1952.	8/1943	1958
330	EKV 930	Guy Arab I 6LW	FD25866	Brush	UL27/28R	Chassis diverted from Middlesbrough CT in exchange for 299.	5/1943	1953
331	EKV 931	Guy Arab II 5LW	FD26227	Park Royal	UH30/26R	Reb Nudd Bros & Lockyer, 1951.	10/1943	1959
332	EKV 932	Guy Arab II 5LW	FD26228	Park Royal	UH30/26R	Reb Bond, Wythenshawe 1953.	10/1943	1958
333	EKV 933	Guy Arab II 5LW	FD26231	Park Royal	UH30/26R	Reb Nudd Bros & Lockyer, 1951.	10/1943	1958
334	EKV 934	Guy Arab II 5LW	FD26307	Park Royal	UH30/26R	Reb Nudd Bros & Lockyer, 1951.	10/1943	1961
335	EKV 935	Guy Arab II 5LW	FD26337	Park Royal	UH30/26R	Reb Nudd Bros & Lockyer, 1951.	11/1943	1961
336 (436)	EKV 936	Daimler CWA6	11581	Duple	UH30/26R	Rebodied Roe H31/27R, 1951.	2/1944	1963

Fleet No.	Regist. No.	Chassis	Chassis No.	Body	Seating	Modifications/ Notes	Year In	Year Out
337 (437)	EKV 937	Daimler CWA6	11582	Duple	UH30/26R	Rebodied Roe H31/27R, 1951.	2/1944	1964
338	EKV 938	Daimler CWA6	11583	Duple	UH30/26R	Reb Nudd Bros & Lockyer, 1951.	2/1944	1958
339	EKV 939	Daimler CWA6	11636	NCME	UH30/26R	Reb CCT 1952.	2/1944	1958
340	EKV 940	Daimler CWA6	11637	NCME	UH30/26R	Reb CCT 1953.	3/1944	1958
341	EKV 941	Daimler CWA6	11638	NCME	UH30/26R	Reb CCT 1952.	3/1944	1963
342	EKV 942	Daimler CWA6	11643	Weymann	UH30/26R	Reb East Lancs, Bridlington 1952.	3/1944	1963
343	EKV 943	Daimler CWA6	11644	Weymann	UH30/26R	Reb Bond, Wythenshawe 1953.	3/1944	1963
344	EKV 944	Daimler CWA6	11652	Weymann	UH30/26R	Reb Bond, Wythenshawe 1952.	2/1944	1964
345	EKV 945	Daimler CWA6	11653	Weymann	UH30/26R	Reb Bond, Wythenshawe 1952.	3/1944	1958
346	EKV 946	Guy Arab II 5LW	FD26406	Park Royal	UH30/26R	Reb Nudd Bros & Lockyer, 1951.	11/1943	1961
347	EKV 947	Daimler CWA6	11646	NCME	UH30/26R	Reb CCT 1952.	5/1944	1963
348	EKV 948	Daimler CWA6	11634	NCME	UH30/26R	Reb CCT 1952.	5/1944	1963
349	EKV 949	Daimler CWA6	11645	NCME	UH30/26R	Reb CCT 1953.	5/1944	1964
350	EKV 950	Daimler CWA6	11633	NCME	UH30/26R	Reb CCT 1951.	6/1944	1958
351	EKV 951	Daimler CWA6	11649	NCME	UH30/26R	Reb CCT 1951.	5/1944	1958
352	EKV 952	Daimler CWA6	11648	NCME	UH30/26R	Reb CCT 1951.	5/1944	1961
353	EKV 953	Daimler CWA6	11647	NCME	UH30/26R	Reb CCT 1952.	5/1944	1958
354	EKV 954	Daimler CWA6	11679	NCME	UH30/26R	Reb CCT 1952.	6/1944	1962
355	EKV 955	Daimler CWA6	11680	NCME	UH30/26R	Reb CCT 1952.	5/1944	1964
356	EKV 956	Daimler CWA6	11681	NCME	UH30/26R	Reb CCT 1952.	6/1944	1963

Fleet No.	Regist. No.	Chassis	Chassis No.	Body	Seating	Modifications/ Notes	Year In	Year Out
357	EKV 957	Guy Arab II 5LW	FD27197	Strachan	UH30/26R	Reb Bond, Wythenshawe 1953.	1/1945	1958
358	EKV 958	Guy Arab II 5LW	FD27214	Strachan	UH30/26R	Reb Nudd Bros & Lockyer, 1951.	1/1945	1961
359	EKV 959	Guy Arab II 5LW	FD27233	Strachan	UH30/26R	Reb Nudd Bros & Lockyer, 1951.	1/1945	1961
360	FDU 60	Guy Arab II 5LW	FD27257	Strachan	UH30/26R	Last Guy Arab II 5LW delivered. Reb Nudd Bros & Lockyer, 1951.	2/1945	1961
361	EKV 961	Daimler CWA6	11949	Brush	UH30/26R	Reb Bond, Wythenshawe 1953.	2/1945	1958
362	EKV 962	Daimler CWA6	11950	Brush	UH30/26R	Reb CCT 1954.	2/1945	
363	EKV 963	Daimler CWA6	11786	Duple	UH30/26R	Rebodied Roe H31/27R, 1951.	8/1944	1958
364	EKV 964	Daimler CWA6	11787	Duple	UH30/26R	Reb Nudd Bros & Lockyer, 1951.	8/1944	1958
365	EKV 965	Daimler CWA6	11788	Duple	UH30/26R	Reb Nudd Bros & Lockyer, 1951.	8/1944	1958
366	EKV 966	Daimler CWA6	11789	Duple	UH30/26R	Rebodied Roe H31/27R, 1951. Preserved.	8/1944	1959
367	EKV 967	Daimler CWA6	11792	Duple	UH30/26R	Rebodied Roe H31/27R, 1951.	8/1944	1964
368	EKV 968	Daimler CWA6	11793	Duple	UH30/26R	Rebodied Roe H31/27R, 1951.	8/1944	1964
369	EKV 969	Daimler CWA6	11794	Duple	UH30/26R	Rebodied Roe H31/27R, 1951.	8/1944	1964
370	EKV 970	Daimler CWA6	11795	Duple	UH30/26R	Reb Nudd Bros & Lockyer, 1951.	8/1944	1964
371	EKV 971	Daimler CWA6	11796	Duple	UH30/26R	Rebodied Roe H31/27R, 1951.	8/1944	1964
372	EKV 972	Daimler CWA6	11800	Duple	UH30/26R	Reb Bond, Wythenshawe 1953.	8/1944	1958
373	FDU 373	Daimler CWA6	12266	Duple	UH30/26R	Rebodied Roe H31/27R, 1951.	8/1945	1963

Fleet No.	Regist. No.	Chassis	Chassis No.	Body	Seating	Modifications/ Notes	Year In	Year Out
374	FDU 374	Daimler CWA6	12267	Duple	UH30/26R	Reb CCT 1947–1953.	8/1945	1958
375	FDU 375	Daimler CWA6	12268	Duple	UH30/26R	Rebodied Roe H31/27R, 1951.	9/1945	1964
376	FDU 376	Daimler CWA6	12275	Duple	UH30/26R	Reb Bond, Wythenshawe 1952.	9/1945	1963
377	FDU 377	Daimler CWA6D	12331	Duple	UH30/26R	Reb Bond, Wythenshawe 1952.	10/1945	1958
378	FDU 378	Daimler CWA6D	12332	Duple	UH30/26R	Reb Bond, Wythenshawe 1952.	10/1945	1963
379	FDU 379	Daimler CWA6D	12333	Duple	UH30/26R	Reb Bond, Wythenshawe 1953.	10/1945	1958
380	FDU 380	Daimler CWA6D	12334	Duple	UH30/26R	Reb Bond, Wythenshawe 1952.	10/1945	1963
381	FDU 381	Daimler CWA6D	12335	Duple	UH30/26R	Reb Nudd Bros & Lockyer, 1951.	11/1945	1958
382	FDU 382	Daimler CWA6D	12349	Duple	UH30/26R	Rebodied Roe H31/27R, 1951.	11/1945	1963
383	FDU 383	Daimler CWA6D	12408	Duple	UH30/26R	Reb Bond, Wythenshawe 1953.	11/1945	1958
384	FDU 384	Daimler CWA6D	12409	Duple	UH30/26R	Rebodied Roe H31/27R, 1951.	11/1945	1984
385	FDU 385	Daimler CWA6D	12596	Duple	UH30/26R	Reb Nudd Bros & Lockyer, 1951.	3/1946	1958
386	FDU 386	Daimler CWA6D	12609	Duple	UH30/26R	Reb Bond, Wythenshawe 1953.	3/1946	1958